# AN ANTHOLOGY OF WAR POEMS

# AN ANTHOLOGY
# OF WAR POEMS

*Compiled by*
FREDERICK BRERETON

*Introduction by*
## EDMUND BLUNDEN

LONDON 48 PALL MALL
## W. COLLINS SONS & CO LTD
GLASGOW SYDNEY AUCKLAND

# CONTENTS

7

9

# THE SOLDIER POETS OF
## 1914-1918

# THE SOLDIER POETS OF
## 1914-1918

" SOLDIER POETS "—the term was a few years ago almost as familiar as a ration-card. The greatest war, breaking all records, produced the greatest number of poets (at least, in the English language) that any war has done. Moreover, on previous occasions of upheaval in Flanders or more remote fields, the poets had been fortunate enough, if not precisely

> *To see what fighting there had been*
> *Quite clearly—on the tape-machine,*

to remain in a clean, quiet, and not much distressed situation. It was one of the romantic things about Thomas Campbell that he had seen as well as sung the Battle of Hohenlinden, or at any rate people said he had seen it, which was remarkable enough. In the early days of the World War, it appeared as though the tradition of poetry might be maintained " with due regard to decent taste," and that lyres would be struck and elegiac business carried on as

13

usual by melodious patriots, seated at their customary tables. Some hard things have been said about these dignified performers. " Alfred Noyes, the conventional Victorian," writes an American anthologist, " turned from peace poems to war poems without batting an eyelash."

It soon became evident, however, that the army (the navy does not seem to have been so vocal) did not intend to have its poetry supplied from the factory. The emotional shock that so bewildering a change of prospect meant to those who enlisted for three years or the duration of the war awoke deeper utterance than men ordinarily need or permit themselves to attempt. At first, speaking broadly, the poetry thus called into existence was concerned with the beauty of English life, made distinct by the act of separation, renunciation. The fact of war was still strange and enigmatic. Whatever war was, almost every one was, as it were, under oath not to make a song about its dreadfulness. Hardly any one could be genuinely, at that early stage, in two minds about it. The appalling destruction which it would ultimately mean, direct and indirect, was not seen ; just as, had you seen a pretty Picard village one bright morning in 1916, you would not have guessed that two days later there would have been nothing but a few mounds, hundreds of large holes, and some tree stumps to represent it. So, the early war poetry is mainly insistent on chivalrous obligation, the things that matter more than death, and the affections and home pictures of the life that the soldier leaves behind him.

Conspicuous among the first poets who had gone to the wars, Rupert Brooke perfected the theme which they mostly had. He was already a man of exalted view and graceful expression. As it chanced, he did not see the war in its later unfoldings, or we might have had from him, as from C. E. Montague in prose, some noble numbers won in disenchantment. His period was that in which, undoubtedly, the romantic note was justified in any being less than an Aeschylus or a Confucius. He did not discern anything more complex in the case than sacrifice for an ideal, consolation for the sacrifice ; what he discerned, that he adorned with a classical manner. Later on it became difficult to read his verse, which nevertheless resumes something of its former effect now.

Another poet who, dying, became famous, was C. H. Sorley. He, too, was denied the opportunity to witness and to condemn at length the war of attrition, and the attrition of war. He began to feel the futility of the argument, the doom of the best of men, before the battle of Loos claimed him in the autumn of 1915. He declared his largeness of spirit in a sonnet *To Germany*, which ends with true prophecy,

> *When it is peace, then we may view again*
> *With new-won eyes each other's truer form*
> *And wonder. Grown more loving-kind and warm*
> *We'll grasp firm hands and laugh at the old pain*
> *When it is peace. But until peace, the storm,*
> *The darkness and the thunder and the rain.*

Sorley, too, perceived how grimly it came about that the man in the trenches was cut off by an impassable gulf from the people at home—from himself a year younger.

> *When you see millions of the mouthless dead*
> *Across your dreams in pale battalions go,*
> *Say not soft things as other men have said,*

*That you'll remember. For you need not so.*
*Give them not praise. For, deaf, how should they*
  *know*
*It is not curses heaped on each gashed head ?*
*Nor tears. Their blind eyes see not your tears flow. . . .*

The main mystery of the Old Front Line was that it created a kind of concord between the combatants, but a discord between them and those who, not being there, kept up the war.

With the multiplying of disastrous attacks, the swelling rage of ever-stiffening masses of artillery, the extension of the ruined areas, the tormenting of periods of rest with night-bombing, the relentless crowding of men into the Golgotha, the cleavage between the fighting man and the civilian, the obscuring of the intention of Englishmen, and, simply, with the disappearance of novelty in bullet and bayonet, the war became a recognised error. In Mr. Robert Graves's *Fairies and Fusiliers*, 1916, may be read examples of the transition of poetry from the first enthusiasms to an attitude of painful questioning. On one page you find *A Renascence*, which looks backward to the spirit of Brooke and admires the event not only because it has made weaklings into athletes but because

> *Of their travailings and groans*
> *Poetry is born again.*

On another page the poetical interest is treated personally :—

> *Here's an end to my art !*
> *I must die and I know it,*
> *With battle murder at my heart—*
> *Sad death for a poet !*

The time was now coming when the attack on war was to be made on a large scale, without egotism or minor concern, by a poet with every qualification for his glorious and difficult crusade. To-day the name of Siegfried Sassoon is perhaps associated by most readers with his finely modulated prose work, the *Memoirs of a Fox-Hunting Man* ; but it was in *The Old Huntsman* of 1917 that he set out, a unique adventurer, to tell the truth about war poetically. I have called this a difficult task ; by way of defining the epithet, the reader will remember that Mr.

Sassoon was still a soldier, that a vast amount of falsehood concerning war and Tommy's smile had been dinned into the public mind, and that the communicating of the unprecedented and solitary miseries of modern battlefields was scarcely within the bounds of hope. As for this author's qualifications, the first was a poetic nature trained in patient watchings for the significant thing and the correspondingly significant phrase ; the second was a happy intimacy with peaceful life, such as had bred affectionate discernment of the beautiful in human character, in customary things, in wild nature, in the arts ; the third was the long acquaintance of this philosophic lyrist with warfare, and with his friend " the average man " in the throes of warfare. *The Old Huntsman* offered portraits of the soldier seen against the dreadful horizons, or lying still on the fatal parapets ; and here were outbursts of white anger against those who drowned all the cryings of truth with clamorous claptrap or vulgar excess. The humour of Mr. Sassoon in his recent memoirs has delighted many ; but they may see what a poet's humour can be like when just indignation commands in *The Old Huntsman*.

Mr. Sassoon proceeded to write and publish in periodicals and loose sheets the fuller statement of, and against, war which appeared in the volume, *Counter-Attack*, in June, 1918. It was his triumph to be the first man who even described war fully and exactly ; and had description been all that he did, the feat would have been distinguished. The face of war is one of protean changes. In order to catch those countenances, a man has to be acute in a rare degree. A fighting man, too, is busy ; the whirlpool of danger, and labour, and noise which has swallowed him is not of a sort to assist him in a plain observant report. No ferocity could deflect the passion in Mr. Sassoon's mind for a complete impression, such as must command the attention and understanding even of the uninitiated, of the fury. He will laugh at the figure, but he was something like one of the figures who stand their ground and draw their swords in the old battle pictures amid the thickening explosions and conflagrations. He contrived to draw a sword for a greater ideal than the colours of a regiment, by recording what war does to " youth and laughter " in poignant epithet and striking verb, in various rhythm and in dramatic narration. He

showed in many passages how life had bloomed to
these men, even when they had been least analytical
of their normality :—

> *I see them in foul dug-outs, gnawed by rats,*
>    *And in the ruined trenches, lashed with rain,*
> *Dreaming of things they did with balls and bats,*
>    *And mocked by hopeless longing to regain*
> *Bank-holidays, and picture shows, and spats,*
>    *And going to the office in the train.*

He showed to what extreme the failure of nations
to think calmly, to consider the obvious, had
withered these men ; he had the power of producing
in a remark or detail the scorching hopelessness in
which they were imprisoned : I italicise,

> *They leave their trenches*, going over the top
> *While* time ticks blank and busy *on their wrists.*

There was one who had been moving in the
direction of this Shelleyan revolutionary (only so,
because conservative wherever the existing thing is
choice and laudable) almost since the beginning of
the war, but who did not discover himself very

quickly. When he did, he instantly showed the power to speak with Mr. Sassoon, and it was his meeting with that poet which released his energies and encouraged him to marshal his magnificent gifts with intellectual control. This young officer was Wilfred Owen, who, apparently apprehending that the war might be protracted far beyond 1918, set himself to strike a blow at it with an organised series of poems. Many of those he completed. Then, in spite of having already had much fiery experience of the shell-holes and drum-fire, he argued that he must return to the field in order not only to help his friend the fighting man as an officer, but also to equip himself with new experience for an un-answerable poetic onslaught upon the war. He was one of the last to be killed, and probably the greatest of those poets who were killed. For his poetical capacity, it is necessary to bring forward the parallel of Keats, whom he adored. He was endowed with a fruitful imagination, distilling itself into the richest cordials of phrases, and with a sense of grand music, that made him explore all known and some unknown harmonies of metre and syllabic sound. But Owen was anything but an æsthetic recluse. He was of an open, ardent, and genial sensibility, profoundly devoted to the happiness and freedom of others, yearning to see each man blessed with whatever honourable pleasure life has to give suited to individual condition. The world in which Owen came to maturity of thought was that which for four years rolled the individual into one red burial. Once he had assured himself by Mr. Sassoon's example that poetry could do much to bring us back to our senses, and that the same powers which can best concentrate the beauty of things can suggest grotesque but actual horror, despair, outrage, and strange passion, he applied himself wholly to that work. What he has written will last ; he has said much that may only be understood by those who were with him, but he had equally perpetuated the general wilderness, the charged atmosphere, the hardly sane constancy of the soldier, the pity which he desired above all to interpret.

I have not crowded this sketch of certain aspects of the war's poets with names ; nor is it necessary to add much regarding the verse which in subsequent years has reflected and re-echoed the years of brilliance and catastrophe. Most of this literature has been in prose, and in protest ; and still there is need for protest, and though *Journey's End* arouse the sympathies of millions from London to Tokyo there is need. We shall be liable to vaingloriousness if we now blame too earnestly the young soldiers of 1914 and 1915 who with their delicate and unreflecting stanzas failed to paint war as it is. They were not experienced, and, at a time when the country needed their sweetness, they gave it. Maybe in the judgment of after years it needed bitterness more ; but to everything there is a season. Equally, we must not be too well satisfied that we are now making, and attending to, effectual and eager complaints against the survival of that false gross idol, War. These have been made through the ages ; and, when all had been forgotten, right out of the mephitic gulf of the bombardment, in prehistoric 1916 and 1917, arose two poets of unshakable resolution, whose protests will not be surpassed for poetic intensity and plan or for selflessness in fighting this world's battles.

EDMUND BLUNDEN.

# AN ANTHOLOGY OF WAR POEMS

## Bombardment

Four days the earth was rent and torn
By bursting steel,
The houses fell about us;
Three nights we dared not sleep,
Sweating, and listening for the imminent crash
Which meant our death.

The fourth night every man,
Nerve-tortured, racked to exhaustion,
Slept, muttering and twitching,
While shells crashed overhead.

The fifth day there came a hush;
We left our holes
And looked above the wreckage of the earth
To where the white clouds moved in silent lines
Across the untroubled blue.

RICHARD ALDINGTON.

## Barrage

Thunder,
The gallop of innumerable Valkyrie impetuous for
  battle,
The beating of vast eagle wings above Prometheus,
The contest of tall barbaric gods smitten by the
  hammer of Thor,
Pursuit! Pursuit! Pursuit!
The huge black dogs of hell
Leaping full-mouthed in murderous pursuit!

RICHARD ALDINGTON.

## Machine Guns

Gold flashes in the dark,
And on the road
Each side, behind, in front of us,
Gold sparks
Where the fierce bullets strike the stones.

In a near shell-hole lies a wounded man,
The stretcher-bearers bending over him;
And at our feet
Cower shrinkingly against the ground
Dark shadowy forms of men.

Only we two stand upright;
All differences of life and character smoothed out
And nothing left
Save that one foolish tie of caste
That will not let us shrink.

RICHARD ALDINGTON.

## A Moment's Interlude

One night I wandered alone from my comrades'
    huts;
The grasshoppers chirped softly
In the warm misty evening;
Bracken fronds beckoned from the darkness
With exquisite frail green fingers;
The tree-gods muttered affectionately about me
And from the distance came the grumble of a
    kindly train.

I was so happy to be alone
So full of love for the great speechless earth,
That I could have laid my cheek in the grasses
And caressed with my lips the hard sinewy body
Of Earth, the cherishing mistress of bitter lovers.

RICHARD ALDINGTON.

## Marthe

Marthe of the lowered eyes;
    Eyes beautiful that seem to dim
    Like violets at the water's rim,
Marthe of the lowered eyes.

Marthe of the pale, pale face;
    That shows the anxious soul's suspense,
    And sorrow veiled by reticence,
Marthe of the pale, pale face.

Marthe of the heart of gold;
    Where hid as in a cloister-cell
    Abides her love for him who fell,
Marthe of the heart of gold.

H. D'A. B.
*Major*, 55*th Division*
(*B.E.F., France*).

## The March

Like lances of a phantom-troop
  The rain sweeps by in level lines
Where stunted pollard-willows droop
  And slag-heaps lift o'er gutted mines.

A sky morose, tempestuous, black,
  The low horizon misty-wan,
And silent o'er the long, long track
  A khaki column trudging on.

Past gaping roofs and tumbled stalls,
  Past dismal yards and hovels damp,
Where eyeless windows mock the walls,
  They march with hollow-thudding tramp.

H. D'A. B.
*Major, 55th Division*
*(B.E.F., France).*

## Givenchy Field

The dead lie on Givenchy field
    As lie the sodden Autumn leaves,
The dead lie on Givenchy field,
    The trailing mist a cerement weaves.

Abandoned, save for murder's work,
    A mine-shaft bulks against the stars,
And fast receding in the mirk
    The trenches show like umber scars.

" All's quiet," the sentry's message runs,
    Outwearied men to slumber yield;
The rain drips down the hooded guns,
    All's quiet upon Givenchy field.

H. D'A. B.
*Major, 55th Division*
*(B.E.F., France).*

## Nox Mortis

The afternoon
 Flutters and dies;
The fairy moon
 Burns in the skies
As they grow darker, and the first stars shine
On Night's rich mantle—purple like warm wine.


On each white road
 Begins to crawl
The heavy toad:
 The night-birds call,
And round the trees the swift bats flit and wheel,
While from the barns the rats begin to steal.


So now must I,
 Bird of the night,
Towards the sky
 Make wheeling flight,
And bear my poison o'er the gloomy land,
And let it loose with hard unsparing hand.


The chafers boom
 With whirring wings,
And haunt the gloom
 Which twilight brings—
So in nocturnal travel do I wail
As through the night the winged engines sail.

Death, Grief, and Pain
　　Are what I give.
　O that the slain
　　Might live—might live!
I know them not, for I have blindly killed,
And nameless hearts with nameless sorrow filled.


　　Thrice cursed War
　　　Which bids that I
　　Such death should pour
　　　Down from the sky.
O, Star of Peace, rise swiftly in the East
That from such slaying men may be released.

PAUL BEWSHER.

# The Dawn Patrol

Sometimes I fly at dawn above the sea,
Where, underneath, the restless waters flow—
   Silver, and cold, and slow.
Dim in the east there burns a new-born sun,
Whose rosy gleams along the ripples run,
   Save where the mist droops low,
Hiding the level loneliness from me.


And now appears beneath the milk-white haze
A little fleet of anchored ships, which lie
   In clustered company,
And seem as they are yet fast bound by sleep,
Although the day has long begun to peep,
   With red-inflamed eye,
Along the still, deserted ocean ways.


The fresh, cold wind of dawn blows on my face
As in the sun's raw heart I swiftly fly,
   And watch the seas glide by.
Scarce human seem I, moving through the skies,
And far removed from warlike enterprise—
   Like some great gull on high
Whose white and gleaming wings bear on through
    space.


Then do I feel with God quite, quite alone,
High in the virgin morn, so white and still,
   And free from human ill:

My prayers transcend my feeble earth-bound
    plaints—
As though I sang among the happy Saints
  With many a holy thrill—
As though the glowing sun were God's bright
    Throne.

My flight is done. I cross the line of foam
That breaks around a town of grey and red,
  Whose streets and squares lie dead
Beneath the silent dawn—then am I proud
That England's peace to guard I am allowed;
  Then bow my humble head,
In thanks to Him Who brings me safely home.

PAUL BEWSHER.

With proud thanksgiving, a mother for
    her children,
    England mourns for her dead across
      the sea.
Flesh of her flesh they were, spirit of
    her spirit,
    Fallen in the cause of the free.


Solemn the drums thrill: Death august
    and royal
    Sings sorrow up into immortal
    spheres.
There is music in the midst of de-
    solation
    And a glory that shines upon our
    tears.


They went with songs to the battle, they
    were young,
    Straight of limb, true of eye, steady
    and aglow.
They were staunch to the end against
    odds uncounted,
    They fell with their faces to the
    foe.

They shall grow not old, as we that are
    left grow old:
  Age shall not weary them, nor the
    years condemn.
At the going down of the sun and in
    the morning
  We will remember them.


They mingle not with their laughing
    comrades again;
  They sit no more at familiar tables
    at home;
They have no lot in our labour of the
    day-time:
  They sleep beyond England's foam.


But where our desires are and our
    hopes profound,
  Felt as a well-spring that is hidden
    from sight,
To the innermost heart of their land
    they are known
  As the stars are known to the
    Night.

As the stars that shall be bright when
we are dust,
Moving in marches upon the
heavenly plain,
As the stars that are starry in the time
of our darkness,
To the end, to the end, they remain.

LAURENCE BINYON.

## Third Ypres

Triumph! How strange, how strong had
    triumph come
On weary hate of foul and endless war
When from its grey gravecloths awoke anew
The summer day. Among the tumbled wreck
Of fascined lines and mounds the light was
    peering,
Half-smiling upon us, and our newfound
    pride;
The terror of the waiting night outlived,
The time too crowded for the heart to count
All the sharp cost in friends killed on the
    assault.
No hook of all the octopus had held us,
Here stood we trampling down the ancient
    tyrant.
So shouting dug we among the monstrous
    pits.

Amazing quiet fell upon the waste,
Quiet intolerable to those who felt
The hurrying batteries beyond the masking
    hills
For their new parley setting themselves in
    array
In crafty fourms unmapped.
                    No, these, smiled faith,
Are dumb for the reason of their overthrow.
They move not back, they lie among the
    crews

Twisted and choked, they'll never speak
    again.
Only the copse where once might stand a
    shrine
Still clacked and suddenly hissed its bullets
    by.
The War would end, the Line was on the
    move,
And at a bound the impassable was passed.
We lay and waited with extravagant joy.


Now dulls the day and chills; comes there no
    word
From those who swept through our new lines
    to flood
The lines beyond ? but little comes, and so
Sure as a runner time himself's accosted.
And the slow moments shake their heavy
    heads,
And croak, " They're done, they'll none of
    them get through,
They're done, they've all died on the entangle-
    ments,
The wire stood up like an unplashed hedge
    and thorned
With giant spikes—and there they've paid the
    bill."


Then comes the black assurance, then the
    sky's
Mute misery lapses into trickling rain,

That wreathes and swims and soon shuts in
 our world.
And those distorted guns, that lay past use,
Why—miracles not over!—all a-firing!
The rain's no cloak from their sharp eyes. And
 you,
Poor signaller, you I passed by this emplace-
 ment,
You whom I warned, poor daredevil, waving
 your flags,
Among this screeching I pass you again and
 shudder
At the lean green flies upon the red flesh
 madding.
Runner, stand by a second. Your message.—
 He's gone,
Falls on a knee, and his right hand uplifted
Claws his last message from his ghostly
 enemy,
Turns stone-like. Well I liked him, that
 young runner,
But there's no time for that. O now for the
 word
To order us flash from these drowning roaring
 traps
And even hurl upon that snarling wire?
Why are our guns so impotent?
       The grey rain,
Steady as the sand in an hour glass on this
 day,
Where through the window the red lilac
 looks,

And all's so still, the chair's odd click is
　　noise—
The rain is all heaven's answer, and with
　　hearts
Past reckoning we are carried into night
And even sleep is nodding here and there.

The second night steals through the shrouding
　　rain.
We in our numb thought crouching long have
　　lost
The mockery triumph, and in every runner
Have urged the mind's eye see the triumph to
　　come,
The sweet relief, the straggling out of hell
Into whatever burrows may be given
For life's recall. Then the fierce destiny
　　speaks.
This was the calm, we shall look back for this.
The hour is come; come, move to the relief!
Dizzy we pass the mule-strewn track where
　　once
The ploughman whistled as he loosed his
　　team;
And where he turned home-hungry on the
　　road,
The leaning pollard marks us hungrier
　　turning.
We crawl to save the remnant who have torn
Back from the tentacled wire, those whom no
　　shell
Has charred into black carcasses—Relief !

They grate their teeth until we take their
    room,
And through the churn of moonless night and
    mud
And flaming burst and sour gas we are
    huddled
Into the ditches where they bawl sense awake,
And in a frenzy that none could reason calm,
(Whimpering some, and calling on the dead)
They turn away: as in a dream they find
Strength in their feet to bear back that strange
    whim
Their body.
            At the noon of the dreadful day
Our trench and death's is on a sudden stormed
With huge and shattering salvoes, the clay
    dances
In founts of clods around the concrete sites,
Where still the brain devises some last armour
To live out the poor limbs.
              This wrath's oncoming
Found four of us together in a pillbox,
Skirting the abyss of madness with light
    phrases,
White and blinking, in false smiles grimacing.
The demon grins to see the game, a moment
Passes, and—still the drum-tap dongs my
    brain
To a whirring void—through the great breach
    above me
The light comes in with icy shock and the rain
Horridly drips. Doctor, talk, talk! if dead

Or stunned I know not; the stinking powdered
  concrete,
The lyddite turns me sick—my hair's all full
Of this smashed concrete.  O I'll drag you,
  friends,
Out of the sepulchre into the light of day,
For this is day, the pure and sacred day.
And while I squeak and gibber over you,
Look, from the wreck a score of field-mice
  nimble,
And tame and curious look about them;
  (these
Calmed me, on these depended my salvation).
There comes my sergeant, and by all the powers
The wire is holding to the right battalion,
And I can speak—but I myself first spoken
Hear a known voice now measured even to
  madness
Call me by name.
              " For God's sake send and help us,
Here in a gunpit, all headquarters done for,
Forty or more, the nine-inch came right
  through,
All splashed with arms and legs, and I myself
The only one not killed nor even wounded.
You'll send—God bless you! " The more
  monstrous fate
Shadows our own, the mind swoons doubly
  burdened,
Taught how for miles our anguish groans and
  bleeds
A whole sweet countryside amuck with murder;

Each moment puffed into a year with death.
Still wept the rain, roared guns,
Still swooped into the swamps of flesh and
    blood,
All to the drabness of uncreation sunk,
And all thought dwindled to a moan, Relieve!
But who with what command can now relieve
The dead men from that chaos, or my soul?

EDMUND BLUNDEN.

# The Zonnebeke Road

Morning, if this late withered light can claim
Some kindred with that merry flame
Which the young day was wont to fling through
    space!
Agony stares from each grey face.
And yet the day is come; stand down! stand down!
Your hands unclasped from rifles while you can;
The frost has pierced them to the bended bone?
Why, see old Stevens there, that iron man,
Melting the ice to shave his grotesque chin!
Go ask him, shall we win?
I never liked this bay, some foolish fear
Caught me the first time that I came in here;
That dugout fallen in awakes, perhaps,
Some formless haunting of some corpse's chaps.
True, and wherever we have held the line,
There were such corners, seeming-saturnine
For no good cause.
                      Now where Haymarket starts,
That is no place for soldiers with weak hearts;
The minenwerfers have it to the inch.
Look, how the snow-dust whisks along the road
Piteous and silly; the stones themselves must flinch
In this east wind; the low sky like a load
Hangs over, a dead-weight. But what a pain
Must gnaw where its clay cheek
Crushes the shell-chopped trees that fang the plain—
The ice-bound throat gulps out a gargoyle shriek.
The wretched wire before the village line
Rattles like rusty brambles or dead bine,

And there the daylight oozes into dun;
Black pillars, those are trees where roadways run.
Even Ypres now would warm our souls; fond fool,
Our tour's but one night old, seven more to cool!
O screaming dumbness, O dull clashing death,
Shreds of dead grass and willows, homes and men,
Watch as you will, men clench their chattering teeth
And freeze you back with that one hope, disdain.

EDMUND BLUNDEN.

## Secret Treaties

We thought to find a cross like Calvary's,
And queened proud England with a diadem
Of thorns.  Impetuous armies clamouring
For war, from the far utterance of the seas
We sprang, to win a new Jerusalem.
Now is our shame, for we have seen you fling
Full-sounding honour from your lips like phlegm
And bargain up our soul in felonies.

O England, it were better men should read,
In dusty chronicles, of how a death
Had found thee in the van of these crusades;
To tell their eager sons with bated breath,
And burning eyes, about a golden deed,
A vanished race, and high immortal Shades.

FREDERICK V. BRANFORD.

## Night Flying

Aloft on footless levels of the night
A pilot thunders through the desolate stars,
Sees in the misty deep a fainting light
Of far-off cities cast in coal-dark bars
Of shore and soundless sea; and he is lone,
Snatched from the universe like one forbid,
Or like a ghost caught from the slay and thrown
Out on the void, nor God cared what he did.

Till from these unlinked whisperers that pain
The buried earth he swings his boat away,
Even as a lonely thinker who hath run
The gamut of greatlore, and found the Inane,
Then stumbles at midnight upon a sun
And all the honour of a mighty day.

FREDERICK V. BRANFORD.

## Over the Dead

Who in the splendour of a simple thought,
Whether for England or her enemies,
Went in the night, and in the morning died;
Each bleeding piece of human earth that lies
Stark to the carrion wind, and groaning cries
For burial—each Jesu crucified—
Hath surely won the thing He dearly bought;
For wrong is right when wrong is greatly wrought.

Yet is the Nazarene no thane of Thor,
To play on partial fields the puppet king,
Bearing the battle down with bloody hand.
Serene He stands, above the gods of war,
A naked man where shells go thundering—
The great unchallenged Lord of No-Man's Land.

FREDERICK V. BRANFORD.

## The Soldier

If I should die, think only this of me:
    That there's some corner of a foreign field
That is for ever England.  There shall be
    In that rich earth a richer dust concealed ;
A dust whom England bore, shaped, made aware ;
    Gave, once, her flowers to love, her ways to roam,
A body of England's breathing English air,
    Washed by the rivers, blest by suns of home.

And think, this heart, all evil shed away,
    A pulse in the eternal mind, no less
        Gives somewhere back the thoughts by
            England given ;
Her sights and sounds ; dreams happy as her day ;
    And laughter, learnt of friends ; and gentleness,
        In hearts at peace, under an English heaven.

RUPERT BROOKE.

## Guns of Verdun

Guns of Verdun point to Metz
From the plated parapets;
Guns of Metz grin back again
O'er the fields of fair Lorraine.

Guns of Metz are long and grey
Growling through a summer day;
Guns of Verdun, grey and long,
Boom an echo of their song.

Guns of Metz to Verdun roar,
" Sisters, you shall foot the score ";
Guns of Verdun say to Metz,
" Fear not, for we pay our debts."

Guns of Metz they grumble, " When ? "
Guns of Verdun answer then,
" Sisters, when to guard Lorraine
Gunners lay you East again! "

P. R. CHALMERS.

# From the Somme

In other days I sang of simple things,
  Of summer dawn, and summer noon and night,
The dewy grass, the dew-wet fairy rings,
    The lark's long golden flight.


Deep in the forest I made melody
  While squirrels cracked their hazel nuts on high,
Or I would cross the wet sand to the sea
    And sing to sea and sky.


When came the silvered silence of the night
  I stole to casements over scented lawns,
And softly sang of love and love's delight
    To mute white marble fauns.


Oft in the tavern parlour I would sing
  Of morning sun upon the mountain vine,
And, calling for a chorus, sweep the string
    In praise of good red wine.


I played with all the toys the gods provide,
  I sang my songs and made glad holiday.
Now I have cast my broken toys aside
    And flung my lute away.

A singer once, I now am fain to weep
  Within my soul I feel strange music swell,
Vast chants of tragedy too deep—too deep
  For my poor lips to tell.

LESLIE COULSON.

*Sergt., London Regiment, R.F.*

(*Died of wounds in France, October,* 1916).

# The Secret

What is the secret—the secret
   That lies at the heart of it all—
The surge of the stars, the cry of the wind,
   And the beat of the sea,
And the surge and the cry, and the beat of the
      soul in me ?

LESLIE COULSON.
*Sergt., London Regiment, R.F.*
(*Died of wounds in France, October,* 1916).

## "On the Wings of the Morning"

A sudden roar, a mighty rushing sound,
 a jolt or two, a smoothly sliding rise,
a tumbled blur of disappearing ground,
  and then all sense of motion slowly dies.
   Quiet and calm, the earth slips past below,
   as underneath a bridge still waters flow.


My turning wing inclines towards the ground;
 the ground itself glides up with graceful swing
and at the plane's far tip twirls slowly round,
  then drops from sight again beneath the wing
   to slip away serenely as before,
   a cubist-patterned carpet on the floor.


Hills gently sink and valleys gently fill.
 The flattened fields grow ludicrously small;
slowly they pass beneath and slower still
  until they hardly seem to move at all.
   Then suddenly they disappear from sight,
   hidden by fleeting wisps of faded white.


The wing-tips, faint and dripping, dimly show,
 blurred by the wreaths of mist that intervene.
Weird, half-seen shadows flicker to and fro
  across the pallid fog-bank's blinding screen.
   At last the choking mists release their hold,
   and all the world is silver, blue, and gold.

The air is clear, more clear than sparkling wine;
   compared with this wine is a turgid brew.
The far horizon makes a clean-cut line
   between the silver and the depthless blue.
     Out of the snow-white level reared on high
     glittering hills surge up to meet the sky.


Outside the wind-screen's shelter gales may
       race:
   but in the seat a cool and gentle breeze
blows steadily upon my grateful face,
   as I sit motionless and at my ease,
     contented just to loiter in the sun
     and gaze around me till the day is done.


And so I sit, half-sleeping, half-awake,
   dreaming a happy dream of golden days,
until at last, with a reluctant shake
   I rouse myself, and with a lingering gaze
     at all the splendour of the shining plain
     make ready to come down to earth again.


The engine stops: a pleasant silence reigns—
   silence, not broken, but intensified
by the soft, sleepy wires' insistent strains,
   that rise and fall, as with a sweeping glide
     I slither down the well-oiled sides of space,
     towards a lower, less enchanted place.

59

The clouds draw nearer, changing as they come.
　　Now, like a flash, fog grips me by the throat.
Down goes the nose: at once the wires' low hum
　　begins to rise in volume and in note,
　　　　till, as I hurtle from the choking cloud
　　　　it swells into a scream, high-pitched, and loud.


The scattered hues and shades of green and brown
　　fashion themselves into the land I know,
turning and twisting, as I spiral down
　　towards the landing ground; till, skimming low,
　　　　I glide with slackening speed across the ground,
　　　　and come to rest with lightly grating sound.

JEFFERY DAY.

## The Turkish Trench Dog

Night held me as I crawled and scrambled near
The Turkish lines.  Above, the mocking stars
Silvered the curving parapet, and clear
Cloud-latticed beams o'erflecked the land with bars;
I, crouching, lay between
Tense-listening armies, peering through the night,
Twin-giants bound by tentacles unseen.
Here in dim-shadowed light
I saw him, as a sudden movement turned
His eyes towards me, glowing eyes that burned
A moment ere his snuffling muzzle found
My trail;  and then as serpents mesmerise
He chained me with those unrelenting eyes,
That muscle-sliding rhythm, knit and bound
In spare-limbed symmetry, those perfect jaws
And soft-approaching pitter-patter paws.
Nearer and nearer like a wolf he crept—
That moment had my swift revolver leapt—
But terror seized me, terror born of shame
Brought flooding revelation.  For he came
As one who offers comradeship deserved,
An open ally of the human race,
And sniffing at my prostrate form unnerved
He licked my face!

GEOFFREY DEARMER.

# Five Souls

### First Soul

I was a peasant of the Polish plain;
I left my plough because the message ran:—
Russia, in danger, needed every man
To save her from the Teuton; and was slain.
*I gave my life for freedom—This I know*
*For those who bade me fight had told me so.*

### Second Soul

I was a Tyrolese, a mountaineer;
I gladly left my mountain home to fight
Against the brutal treacherous Muscovite;
And died in Poland on a Cossack spear.
*I gave my life for freedom—This I know*
*For those who bade me fight had told me so.*

### Third Soul

I worked in Lyons at my weaver's loom,
When suddenly the Prussian despot hurled
His felon blow at France and at the world;
Then I went forth to Belgium and my doom.
*I gave my life for freedom—This I know*
*For those who bade me fight had told me so.*

### Fourth Soul

I owned a vineyard by the wooded Main,
Until the Fatherland, begirt by foes
Lusting her downfall, called me, and I rose
Swift to the call—and died in far Lorraine.
*I gave my life for freedom—This I know*
*For those who bade me fight had told me so.*

### Fifth Soul

I worked in a great shipyard by the Clyde;
There came a sudden word of wars declared,
Of Belgium, peaceful, helpless, unprepared,
Asking our aid: I joined the ranks, and died.
*I gave my life for freedom—This I know*
*For those who bade me fight had told me so.*

W. N. EWER.

And now, while the dark vast earth shakes
    and rocks
In this wild dream-like snare of mortal
    shocks,
How look (I muse) those cold and solitary
    stars
On these magnificent, cruel wars ?—
Venus, that brushes with her shining lips
(Surely!) the wakeful edge of the world
    and mocks
With hers its all ungentle wantonness ?—
Or the large moon (pricked by the spars
    of ships
Creeping and creeping in their restlessness),
The moon pouring strange light on things
    more strange,
Looks she unheedfully on seas and lands
Trembling with change and fear of counter-
    change ?

O, not earth trembles, but the stars, the
    stars!
The sky is shaken and the cool air is
    quivering.
I cannot look up to the crowded height
And see the fair stars trembling in their
    light,
For thinking of the star-like spirits of men
Crowding the earth and with great passion
    quivering :—

Stars quenched in anger and hate, stars
    sick with pity.
I cannot look up to the naked skies
Because a sorrow on dark midnight lies,
Death, on the living world of sense;
Because on my own land a shadow lies
That may not rise:
Because from bare grey hillside and rich
    city
Streams of uncomprehending sadness
    pour,
Thwarting the eager spirit's pure intelli-
    gence . . .
How look (I muse) those cold and
    solitary stars
On these magnificent, cruel wars ?


Stars trembled in broad heaven, faint
    with pity.
An hour to dawn I looked. Beside the
    trees
Wet mist shaped other trees that branch-
    ing rose,
Covering the woods and putting out the
    stars.
There was no murmur on the seas,
No wind blew—only the wandering air
    that grows
With dawn, then murmurs, sighs,
And dies.
The mist climbed slowly, putting out the
    stars,

And the earth trembled when the stars
    were gone;
And moving strangely everywhere upon
The trembling earth, thickened the
    watery mist.

And for a time the holy things are veiled.
England's wise thoughts are swords ;
    her quiet hours
Are trodden underfoot like wayside
    flowers,
And every English heart is England's
    wholly.
In starless night
A serious passion streams the heaven with
    light.
A common beating is in the air —
The heart of England throbbing every-
    where.
And all her roads are nerves of noble
    thought,
And all her people's brain is but her
    brain ;
And all her history, less her shame,
Is part of her requickened consciousness.
Her courage rises clean again.

Even in victory there hides defeat ;
The spirit's murdered though the body
    survives,
Except the cause for which a people
    strives

Burn with no covetous, foul heat.
Fights she against herself who infamously
　　draws
The sword against man's secret spiritual
　　laws.
But thou, England, because a bitter heel
Hath sought to bruise the brain, the
　　sensitive will,
The conscience of the world,
For this, England, art risen, and shalt
　　fight
Purely through long profoundest night,
Making their quarrel thine who are
　　grieved like thee;
And (if to thee the stars yield victory)
Tempering their hate of the great foe
　　that hurled
Vainly her strength against the conscience
　　of the world.


I looked again, or dreamed I looked, and
　　saw
The stars again and all their peace again.
The moving mist had gone, and shining
　　still
The moon went high and pale above the
　　hill.
Not now those lights were trembling in
　　the vast
Ways of the nervy heaven, nor trembled
　　earth:

Profound and calm they gazed as the
   soft-shod hours passed.
And with less fear (not with less awe,
Remembering, England, all the blood
   and pain)
How look, I cried, you stern and solitary
   stars
On these disastrous wars!

                          JOHN FREEMAN.
*August*, 1914.

## Youth's Own

Out of the fields I see them pass,
    Youth's own battalion—
Like moonlight ghosting over grass—
    To dark oblivion.

They have a wintry march to go—
    Bugle and fife and drum!
With music, softer than the snow
    All flurrying, they come!

They have a bivouac to keep
    Out on a starry heath;
To fling them down, and sleep and sleep
    Beyond reveilly—Death!

Since Youth has vanished from our eyes,
    Who, living, glad can be?
Who will be grieving, when he dies
    And leaves this Calvary?

JOHN GALSWORTHY.

## The Bells of Peace

Lilies are here, tall in the garden bed,
    And on the moor are still the buds of
        May;
Roses are here—and, tolling for our dead,
    The Bells of Peace make summer
        holiday.

And do *they* hear, who in their spring-
        time went ?
    The young, the brave young, leaving
        all behind,
All of their home, love, laughter and
        content,
    The village sweetness and the western
        wind.

Leaving the quiet trees and the cattle red,
    The southern soft mist over granite
        tor—
Whispered from life, by secret valour led
    To face the horror that their souls
        abhor.

Here in the starlight to the owl's " To-
        Whoo! "
    They wandered once; they wander
        still, maybe,
Dreaming of home, clinging the long
        night thro'
    To sound and sight fastened in memory.

Here in the sunlight and the bracken
    green—
  Wild happy roses starring every lane—
Eager to reach the good that might have
    been,
  They *were* at peace. Are they at peace
    again ?

Bells of remembrance, on this summer's
    eve
  Of our relief, Peace and Goodwill ring
    in !
Ring out the Past, and let not Hate
    bereave
  Our dreaming dead of all they died to
    win !

JOHN GALSWORTHY.

## To the Rats

O loathsome rodent with your endless squeaking
You hurry to and fro and give no peace,
Above the noise of Hun projectiles' shrieking
The sound of scratching footfalls never cease.

There is a thing which I could never pen,
The horror with which I regard your race,
For how can I describe my feelings when
I wake and find you sitting on my face.

Oh, how shall I portray the depths I plumb
When, stretched upon this bed, my body numb,
I see you, agile, helter-skelter fly.

Oh, Ignominy! while I sleepless lie,
You play your foolish games with eager zest
And sport and gambol freely on my chest.

E. J. L. GARSTON.
*Lieut., 12th Battalion, Middlesex*
*Regiment (B.E.F.)*

## The Joke

He'ld even have his joke
   While we were sitting tight,
And so he needs must poke
   His silly head in sight
To whisper some new jest
   Chortling, but as he spoke
A rifle cracked . . .
And now God knows when I shall hear the rest!

WILFRED WILSON GIBSON.

## Lament

We who are left, how shall we look again
Happily on the sun or feel the rain
Without remembering how they who went
Ungrudgingly and spent
Their lives for us loved, too, the sun and rain ?

A bird among the rain-wet lilac sings—
But we, how shall we turn to little things
And listen to the birds and winds and streams
Made holy by their dreams,
Nor feel the heart-break in the heart of things ?

WILFRED WILSON GIBSON.

## Summer and Sorrow

Brier rose and woodbine flaunting by the wayside,
    Field afoam with ox-eyes, crowfoot's flaming gold,
Poppies in the corn-rig, broom on every braeside,
    Once again 'tis summer as in years of old—
    Only in my bosom lags the winter's cold.

All among the woodland hyacinths are gleaming;
    O the blue of heaven glinting through the trees!
Lapped in noonday languor Nature lies a-dreaming,
    Lulled to rest by droning clover-haunting bees.
    (Deeper dreams my dear love, slain beyond the
      seas.)

Lost against the sunlight happy larks are singing,
    Lowly list their loved ones nestled in the plain;
Bright about my pathway butterflies are winging,
    Fair and fleet as moments mourned for now in
      vain—
    In my eyes the shadow, at my heart the pain.

A. B. GILLESPIE.

*July*, 28, 1915.

## Corporal Stare

Back from the line one night in June,
I gave a dinner at Béthune—
Seven courses, the most gorgeous meal
Money could buy or batman steal.
Five hungry lads welcomed the fish
With shouts that nearly cracked the
      dish;
Asparagus came with tender tops,
Strawberries in cream, and mutton chops.
Said Jenkins, as my hand he shook,
" They'll put this in the history book."
We bawled Church anthems *in choro*
Of Bethlehem and Hermon snow,
With drinking songs, a mighty sound
To help the good red Pommard round.
Stories and laughter interspersed,
We drowned a long La Bassée thirst—
Trenches in June make throats damned
      dry—
Then through the window suddenly,
Badge, stripes and medals all complete,
We saw him swagger up the street,
Just like a live man—Corporal Stare!
Stare! killed last month at Festubert,
Caught on patrol near the Boche wire,
Torn horribly by machine-gun fire!
He paused, saluted smartly, grinned
Then passed away like a puff of wind,
Leaving us blank astonishment.
The song broke, up we started, leant

Out of the window—nothing there,
Not the least shadow of Corporal Stare,
Only a quiver of smoke that showed
A fag-end dropped on the silent road.

ROBERT GRAVES.

## Two Fusiliers

And have we done with War at last ?
Well, we've been lucky devils both,
And there's no need of pledge or oath
To bind our lovely friendship fast,
By firmer stuff
Close bound enough.

By wire and wood and stake we're bound,
By Fricourt and by Festubert,
By whipping rain, by the sun's glare,
By all the misery and loud sound,
By a Spring day,
By Picard clay.

Show me the two so closely bound
As we, by the wet bond of blood,
By friendship blossoming from mud,
By Death: we faced him, and we found
Beauty in Death,
In dead men, breath.

ROBERT GRAVES.

## Into Battle

The naked earth is warm with Spring,
 And with green grass and bursting
  trees
Leans to the sun's gaze glorying,
 And quivers in the sunny breeze;
And Life is Colour and Warmth and
  Light,
 And a striving evermore for these;
And he is dead who will not fight;
 And who dies fighting has increase.


The fighting man shall from the sun
 Take warmth and life from the glow-
  ing earth;
Speed with the light-foot winds to run,
 And with the trees to newer birth;
And find, when fighting shall be done,
 Great rest, and fullness after dearth.


All the bright company of Heaven
 Hold him in their high comradeship,
The Dog-Star and the Sisters Seven,
 Orion's Belt and sworded hip.


The woodland trees that stand together,
 They stand to him each one a friend,
They gently speak in the windy weather;
 They guide to valley and ridges' end.

The kestrel hovering by day,
   And the little owls that call by night,
Bid him be swift and keen as they,
   As keen of ear, as swift of sight.


The blackbird sings to him, " Brother,
      brother,
   If this be the last song you shall sing
Sing well, for you may not sing another;
   Brother, sing."


In dreary, doubtful, waiting hours,
   Before the brazen frenzy starts,
The horses show him nobler powers;
   O patient eyes, courageous hearts!


And when the burning moment breaks,
   And all things else are out of mind,
And only Joy of Battle takes
   Him by the throat, and makes him
      blind—


Through joy and blindness he shall
      know,
   Not caring much to know, that still,
Nor lead nor steel shall reach him, so
   That it be not the Destined Will.

The thundering line of battle stands,
 And in the air Death moans and sings;
But Day shall clasp him with strong
  hands,
 And Night shall fold him in soft
  wings.

JULIAN GRENFELL.

## To the Poet Before Battle

Now, youth, the hour of thy dread passion comes:
Thy lovely things must all be laid away;
And thou, as others, must face the riven day
Unstirred by rattle of the rolling drums,
Or bugles' strident cry. When mere noise numbs
The sense of being, the fear-sick soul doth sway,
Remember thy great craft's honour, that they
    may say
Nothing in shame of poets. Then the crumbs
Of praise the little versemen joined to take
Shall be forgotten: then they must know we are,
For all our skill in words, equal in might
And strong of mettle as those we honoured; make
The name of poet terrible in just war,
And like a crown of honour upon the fight.

Ivor Gurney.

## To M. M. S.

O may these days of pain,
   These wasted-seeming days,
Somewhere reflower again
   With scent and savour of praise,
Draw out of memory all bitterness
   Of night with Thy sun's rays.

And strengthen Thou in me
   The love of men here found,
And eager charity,
   That, out of difficult ground,
Spring like flowers in barren deserts, or
   Like light, or a lovely sound.

A simpler heart than mine
   Might have seen beauty clear
When I could see no sign
   Of Thee, but only fear.
Strengthen me, make me to see
   Thy beauty always
In every happening here.

IVOR GURNEY.

*In Trenches, March,* 1917.

# In Time of " The Breaking of Nations "

*Thou art my battle-axe and weapons of war : for with thee will I break in pieces the nations, and with thee will I destroy kingdoms.—Jer. li. 20.*

### I

Only a man harrowing clods
   In a slow silent walk
With an old horse that stumbles and nods
   Half asleep as they stalk.

### II

Only thin smoke without flame
   From the heaps of couch-grass:
Yet this will go onward the same
   Though Dynasties pass.

### III

Yonder a maid and her wight
   Come whispering by:
War's annals will cloud into night
   Ere their story die.

THOMAS HARDY.

## Gonnehem

Of Gonnehem it shall be said
That we arrived there late and worn
With marching, and were given a bed
Of lovely straw. And then at morn
On rising from deep sleep saw dangle—
Shining in the sun to spangle,
The all-blue heaven—branchloads of red
Bright cherries which we bought to eat,
Dew-wet, dawn-cool, and sunny-sweet.
There was a tiny court-yard too,
Wherein one shady walnut grew.
Unruffled peace the farm encloses—
I wonder if beneath that tree,
The meditating hens still be.
Are the white walls now gay with roses ?
Does the small fountain yet run free ?
I wonder if the dog still dozes. . . .
Some day we must go back to see.

F. W. Harvey.

## Epitaph

A shallow trench for one so tall!
" Heads down "—no need for that old call
    Beneath the upturned sod.
Safe lies his body, never fret,
Behind that crumpled parapet,
And over all this wind and wet
    His soul sits safe with God.

F. W. HARVEY.

T.D., 13/3/16.

## The Stranger

It happened in a blood-red hell ringed round with
    golden weather;
Walking in khaki through a trench he came,
When life was death, and wounded men and great
    shells screamed together:
I did not know his name,
But so white-faced and wan, we talked a little while
    together
Amongst dead men, and timbers black with flame.

" What would you do with life again," asks he, " if
    one could give it ? "
" No use to talk when life is done," I say.
" But, by the living God, if He should grant me
    life I'd live it
Kinder to man, truer to God each day."

Flame and the noise of doom devoured the words,
    and for a while
Senseless I lay. . . . Then,
Oh, then as in a dream I saw the stranger with a
    smile
Moving towards me over the dead men.

Red, red were his hands and feet and a great hole
    in his side,
Yet glory seemed to blaze about his head;
" Kinder to man, truer to God," he whispered, and
    then died;
Falling down, arms outspread.

Ere darkness fell upon me with the faintness and
    the pain,
I saw a mangled body lying prone
Upon the earth beside me.  But what I can't explain
Is—*The stretcher-bearers found me quite alone.*

But, howsoe'er it happened, it matters not at last,
Since God's dear Son came down to earth and died
In bloodshed, and the darkness of clouds that
    groaned aghast;
With pierced hands and a great wound in His side.
It is not in my heart to hate the pleasant sins I leave
Earth's passion flames within me fierce and strong.
But this is like a shadow ever rising up to thieve
Sin's pleasures, and the lure of every pattern lust
    can weave,
And charm of all things that can do Him wrong.

F. W. HARVEY.

## To the Devil on His Appalling Decadence

Satan, old friend and enemy of man;
Lord of the shadows and the sins whereby
We wretches glimpse the sun in Virtue's sky
Guessing at last the wideness of His plan
Who fashioned kid and tiger, slayer and slain,
The paradox of evil, and the pain
Which threshes joy as with a winnowing fan:

Satan, of old your custom 'twas at least
To throw an apple to the soul you caught
Robbing your orchard. You, before you wrought
Damnation due and marked it with the beast,
Before its eyes were e'en disposed to dangle
Fruitage delicious. And you would not mangle
Nor maul the body of the dear deceased.

But you were called familiarly " Old Nick "—
The Devil, yet a gentleman you know!
Relentless—true, yet courteous to a foe.
Man's soul your traffic was. You would not kick
His bloody entrails flying in the air.
Oh, " Krieg ist Krieg," we know, and " C'est la
　　guerre! "
But Satan, don't you feel a trifle sick ?

F. W. HARVEY.

## After the Battle

So they are satisfied with our Brigade
    And it remains to parcel out the bays!
And we shall have the usual Thanks Parade,
    The beaming General, and the soapy praise.


You will come up in your capacious car
    To find your heroes sulking in the rain,
To tell us how magnificent we are,
    And how you hope we'll do the same again.


And we, who knew your old abusive tongue,
    Who heard you hector us a week before,
We who have bled to boost you up a rung—
    A K.C.B. perhaps, perhaps a Corps—


We who must mourn those spaces in the Mess,
    And somehow fill those hollows in the heart,
We do not want your Sermon on Success,
    Your greasy benisons on Being Smart.


We only want to take our wounds away
    To some warm village where the tumult
    ends,
And drowsing in the sunshine many a day,
    Forget our aches, forget that we had friends.

Weary we are of blood and noise and pain;
  This was a week we shall not soon forget;
And if, indeed, we have to fight again,
  We little wish to think about it yet.


We have done well; we like to hear it said.
  Say it, and then, for God's sake, say no more.
Fight, if you must, fresh battles far ahead,
  But keep them dark behind your château door!

                                A. P. HERBERT.

## Salonika in November

Up above the grey hills the wheeling birds are
    calling,
    Round about the cold grey hills in never-resting
    flight;
Far along the marshes a drifting mist is falling,
    Scattered tents and sandy plain melt into the night.

Round about the grey hills rumbles distant thunder,
    Echoes of the mighty guns firing night and day,—
Grey guns, long guns, that smite the hills asunder,
    Grumbling and rumbling, and telling of the fray.

Out among the islands twinkling lights are glowing,
    Distant little fairy lights, that gleam upon the bay;
All along the broken road grey transport wagons
    going
    Up to where the long grey guns roar and crash
    alway.

Up above the cold grey hills the wheeling birds are
    crying,
    Brother calls to brother, as they pass in restless
    flight.
Lost souls, dead souls, voices of the dying,
    Circle o'er the hills of Greece and wail into the
    night.

BRIAN HILL.
*Second Lieut., Durham Light
Infantry.*

## The Beach Road by the Wood

I know a beach road,
    A road where I would go,
It runs up northward
    From Cooden Bay to Hoe;
And there, in the High Woods,
    Daffodils grow.


And whoever walks along there
    Stops short and sees,
By the moist tree-roots
    In a clearing of the trees,
Yellow great battalions of them,
    Blowing in the breeze.


While the spring sun brightens,
    And the dull sky clears,
They blow their golden trumpets,
    Those golden trumpeteers!
They blow their golden trumpets
    And they shake their glancing spears.


And all the rocking beech-trees
    Are bright with buds again,
And the green and open spaces
    Are greener after rain,
And far to southward one can hear
    The sullen, moaning rain.

Once before I die
   I will leave the town behind,
The loud town, the dark town
   That cramps and chills the mind,
And I'll stand again bareheaded there
   In the sunlight and the wind.

Yes, I shall stand
   Where as a boy I stood
Above the dykes and levels
   In the beach road by the wood,
And I'll smell again the sea breeze,
   Salt and harsh and good.

And there shall rise to me
   From that consecrated ground
The old dreams, the lost dreams
   That years and cares have drowned:
Welling up within me
   And above me and around
The song that I could never sing
   And the face I never found.

GEOFFREY HOWARD.<br>
Lieut., Royal Fusiliers.

## "Without Shedding of Blood . . ."

God gave us England from of old,
But we held light the gift He gave;
Our royal birthright we have sold,
And now the land we lost for gold
    Only our blood can save.


    *Not till thousands have been slain*
    *Shall the green wood be green again ;*
    *Not till men shall fall and bleed*
    *Can brown ale taste like ale indeed.*
    *Blood and blood must yet be shed*
        *To make the roses red.*


For minds made vile, and blind with greed,
For sins that spread from sire to son;
For loss of honour, loss of creed,
There yet remains one cure indeed—
    And there remains but one.


    *Malvern men must die and kill*
    *That wind may blow on Malvern Hill;*
    *Devonshire blood must fall like dew*
    *That Devon's bays may yet be blue;*
    *London must spill out lives like wine*
        *That London's lights may shine.*

Lord, for the years of ease and vice,
For hearts unmanned and souls decayed,
Thou hast required a sacrifice—
A bitter and a bloody price—
   And lo! the price is paid.

*We have given all things that were ours,*
*So that our weeds might yet be flowers ;*
*We have covered half the earth with gore*
*That our houses might be homes once more ;*
*The sword Thou hast demanded, Lord :*
   *And, now, behold the sword !*

GEOFFREY HOWARD.
*Lieut., Royal Fusilier.*

## England

Her seed is sown about the world.  The seas
For Her have path'd their waters.  She is known
In swamps that steam about the burning zone,
And dreaded in the last white lands that freeze.
For Her the glory that was Nineveh's
Is nought: the pomp of Tyre and Babylon
Nought: and for all the realms that Cæsar won—
One tithe of hers were more than all of these.

And she is very small and very green
And full of little lanes all dense with flowers
That wind along and lose themselves between
Mossed farms, and parks, and fields of quiet sheep.
And in the hamlets, where her stalwarts sleep,
Low bells chime out from old elm-hidden towers.

GEOFFREY  HOWARD.
*Lieut., Royal Fusiliers.*

## The Iron Music

The French guns roll continuously
And our guns, heavy, slow;
Along the Ancre, sinuously,
The transport wagons go,
And the dust is on the thistles
And the larks sing up on high . . .
*But I see the Golden Valley*
*Down by Tintern on the Wye.*

For it's just nine weeks last Sunday
Since we took the Chepstow train,
And I'm wondering if one day
We shall do the like again;
For the four-point-two's come screaming
Thro' the sausages on high;
*So there's little use in dreaming*
*How we walked above the Wye.*

Dust and corpses in the thistles
Where the gas-shells burst like snow,
And the shrapnel screams and whistles
On the Bécourt road below,
And the High Wood bursts and bristles
Where the mine-clouds foul the sky . . .
*But I'm with you up at Wyndcroft,*
*Over Tintern on the Wye.*

FORD MADOX HUEFFER.

*Albert, 22/7/16.*

# A Solis Ortus Cardine . . .

Oh, quiet peoples sleeping bed by bed
Beneath grey roof-trees in the glimmering West,
We who can see the silver grey and red
Rise over No Man's Land—salute your rest.

Oh, quiet comrades, sleeping in the clay
Beneath a turmoil you need no more mark,
We who have lived through yet another day
Salute your graves at setting in of dark.

And rising from your beds or from the clay
You, dead, or far from lines of slain and slayers,
Thro' your eternal or your finite day
Give us your prayers!

FORD MADOX HUEFFER.

*Ypres Salient*, 6/9/16.

## "For All We Have and Are"

For all we have and are,
For all our children's fate,
Stand up and meet the war,
The Hun is at the gate!
Our world has passed away
In wantonness o'erthrown.
There is nothing left to-day
But steel and fire and stone!
    Though all we knew depart,
    The old commandments stand:
    " In courage keep your heart,
    In strength lift up your hand."


Once more we hear the word
That sickened earth of old:—
" No law except the Sword
Unsheathed and uncontrolled."
Once more it knits mankind,
Once more the nations go
To meet and break and bind
A crazed and driven foe.


Comfort, content, delight,
The ages' slow-bought gain,
They shrivelled in a night,
Only ourselves remain
To face the naked days
In silent fortitude

Through perils and dismays
Renewed and re-renewed.
Though all we made depart,
The old commandments stand:—
" In patience keep your heart,
In strength lift up your hand."

No easy hopes or lies
Shall bring us to our goal,
But iron sacrifice
Of body, will, and soul.
There is but one task for all—
For each one life to give.
Who stands if freedom fall ?
Who dies if England live ?

RUDYARD KIPLING.

1914.

## In France

The silence of maternal hills
Is round me in my evening dreams;
And round me music-making rills
And mingling waves of pastoral streams.

Whatever way I turn I find
The path is old unto me still.
The hills of home are in my mind,
And there I wander as I will.

FRANCIS LEDWIDGE.

*February* 3, 1917.

## In Flanders Fields

In Flanders fields the poppies blow
Between the crosses, row on row,
 That mark our place; and in the sky
 The larks, still bravely singing, fly
Scarce heard amid the guns below.

We are the Dead.  Short days ago
We lived, felt dawn, saw sunset glow,
 Loved and were loved, and now we lie
  In Flanders fields.

Take up our quarrel with the foe:
To you from failing hands we throw
 The torch; be yours to hold it high.
 If ye break faith with us who die
We shall not sleep, though poppies grow
  In Flanders fields.

JOHN McCRAE.

The Teuton sang the " Wacht am Rhein "
   And " Lieber Augustin," while we
Had " Long, long Trail " and " Clementine "
   And " Old Kit Bag " (to give but three);
   Good songs and yet you must agree,
The Poilu's theme was richer, vaster,
   —Double-distilled felicity!—
" He has been duped—the station-master! "


A joyous thought, an anodyne
   For gelignite and T.N.T.:
A song to cure those saturnine
   Red singing-men of Battersea;
   And, whosoever wrote it, he
Deserves a tomb of alabaster
   Graven on which these words should be:—
" He has been duped—the station-master! "


When I am tired of Gertrude Stein
   (" She said she said that she said she . . ." !)
When the expressionistic line
   Has palled, and Sitwells weary me,
   When bored with psycho-prosody,
Obscurist and grammaticaster
   Give me that song of Picardy:—
" He has been duped—the station-master! "

Prince, did you hear the soldiery
Singing of that obscure disaster—
  (Zenith of Gallic pleasantry)
" He has been duped—the station-master! "

H. S. MACKINTOSH.

## Two Julys

I was so vague in 1914; tossed
    Upon too many purposes, and worthless;
Moody; to this world or the other lost,
    Essential nowhere; without calm and mirthless.
And now I have gained for many ends,
    See my straight road stretch out so white, so
      slender,
That happy road, the road of all my friends,
    Made glad with peace, and holy with surrender.

Proud, proud we fling to the winds of Time our
      token,
    And in our need there wells in us the power,
Given England's swords to keep her honour clean.
Which they shall be which pierce, and which be
      broken,
    We know not, but we know that every hour
We must shine brighter, take an edge more keen.

CHARLES JOHN BEECH MASEFIELD.

*M.C., Acting Capt., 5th North Staffs. Regt.*

*(Killed in Action, July, 1917).*

*July,* 1915.

## Before Action

By all the glories of the day,
And the cool evening's benison:
By the last sunset touch that lay
Upon the hills when day was done:
By beauty lavishly outpoured,
And blessings carelessly received,
By all the days that I have lived,
Make me a soldier, Lord.

By all of all men's hopes and fears
And all the wonders poets sing,
The laughter of unclouded years,
And every sad and lovely thing:
By the romantic ages stored
With high endeavour that was his,
By all his mad catastrophes,
Make me a man, O Lord.

I, that on my familiar hill
Saw with uncomprehending eyes
A hundred of Thy sunsets spill
Their fresh and sanguine sacrifice,
Ere the sun swings his noonday sword
Must say good-bye to all of this:—
By all delights that I shall miss,
Help me to die, O Lord.

" EDWARD MELBOURNE."
(W. N. Hodgson, M.C)
*Lieut., Devon Regiment.*
(*Killed in the Somme Advance, July,* 1916.)

## An April Song

Orchard land! Orchard land!
  Damson blossom, primrose bloom:
Avon, like a silver band
  Winds from Stratford down to Broome:
    All the orchards shimmer white
    For an April day's delight:
    We have risen in our might,
    Left this land we love, to fight,
Fighting still, that these may stand,
    Orchard land! Orchard land!


Running stream! Running stream !
  Ruddy tench and silver perch:
Shakespeare loved the water's gleam
  Sparkling on by Welford church:
    Water fay meets woodland gnome
    Where the silver eddies foam
    Thro' the richly scented loam:
    We are fain to see our home,
See again thy silver gleam,
Running stream! Running stream!


Silver throats! Silver throats!
  Piping blackbird, trilling thrush:
Shakespeare heard your merry notes;
  Still you herald morning's blush:

You shall sing your anthems grand
When we've finished what He planned,
God will hear and understand,
God will give us back our land
Where the water-lily floats,
Silver throats! Silver throats!

GEORGE C. MICHAEL.
*Lance-Corporal, R.E.*

*Written on leave at Stratford-on-Avon.*

## The Nurse

Here in the long white ward I stand,
    Pausing a little breathless space,
Touching a restless fevered hand,
    Murmuring comfort's commonplace—

Long enough pause to feel the cold
    Fingers of fear about my heart;
Just for a moment, uncontrolled,
    All the pent tears of pity start.

While here I strive, as best I may,
    Strangers' long hours of pain to ease,
Dumbly I question—*Far away*
    *Lies my beloved even as these ?*

MISS G. M. MITCHELL.

*August*, 30, 1916.

## Commandeered

Last year he drew the harvest home
  Along the winding upland lane,
The children twisted marigolds
  And clover flowers to deck his mane.
    Last year he drew the harvest home.

To-day, with puzzled, patient face,
  With ears a-droop and weary feet
He marches to the sound of drums
  And draws the gun along the street.
    To-day he draws the guns of war!

L. G. MOBERLEY.

## The Flower of Battle

The summer twilight gently yields
    To star-sown luminous night, and close
The flowers in these Flemish Fields
    Are folded, still the leaves repose;

But as the colour leaves the sky,
    And darkness wraps a suffering earth,
Clamouring, climbing endlessly
    Another blossom springs to birth:

The Flower of Battle, down the wide
    Horizon mantles, tendrils spread,
Its far-flung petals brilliant dyed,
    Yellow, and blinding white, and red.

Fed with our bodies at its root,
    Fed with our hearts its living flame,
It sways in wonder absolute,
    And Flower of Battle is its name. . . .

Men will gaze, awestruck, men will strive
    To reach its glowing heart . . . and some
May turn away while yet alive,
    But few from out its shade may come!

                    R. H. MOTTRAM.

# The Dead Soldier

Thy dear brown eyes which were as depths where
  truth
  Lay bowered with frolic joy, but yesterday
Shone with the fire of thy so guileless youth,
  Now ruthless death has dimmed and closed for
  aye.

Those sweet red lips, that never knew the stain
  Of angry words or harsh, or thoughts unclean,
Have sung their last gay song.  Never again
  Shall I the harvest of their laughter glean.

The goodly harvest of thy laughing mouth
  Is garnered in; and lo! the golden grain
Of all thy generous thoughts, which knew no drouth
  Of meanness, and thy tender words remain

Stored in my heart; and though I may not see
  Thy peerless form nor hear thy voice again,
The memory lives of what thou wast to me.
  We knew great love. . . . We have not lived in
  vain.

SYDNEY OSWALD.
*Major, King's Royal Rifle Corps.*

## Dulce et Decorum Est

Bent double, like old beggars under sacks,
Knock-kneed, coughing like hags, we cursed
    through sludge,
Till on the haunting flares we turned our backs,
And towards our distant rest began to trudge.
Men marched asleep. Many had lost their boots,
But limped on, blood-shod. All went lame, all
    blind;
Drunk with fatigue; deaf even to the hoots
Of gas-shells dropping softly behind.

Gas! Gas! Quick, boys!—An ecstasy of fumbling
Fitting the clumsy helmets just in time,
But some one still was yelling out and stumbling
And flound'ring like a man in fire or lime.
Dim through the misty panes and thick green
    light,
As under a green sea, I saw him drowning.

In all my dreams before my helpless sight,
He plunges at me, guttering, choking, drowning.

If in some smothering dreams, you too could pace
Behind the wagon that we flung him in,
And watch the white eyes wilting in his face,
His hanging face, like a devil's sick of sin,
If you could hear, at every jolt, the blood
Come gargling from the froth-corrupted lungs
Bitten as the cud

Of vile, incurable sores on innocent tongues,—
My friend, you would not tell with such high zest
To children ardent for some desperate glory,
The old Lie: *Dulce et decorum est
Pro patria mori.*

WILFRED OWEN.

## Parable of the Old Men and the Young

So Abram rose, and clave the wood, and went
And took the fire with him, and a knife.
And as they sojourned both of them together,
Isaac the first-born spake and said, My Father,
Behold the preparations, fire and iron,
But where the lamb for this burnt offering ?
Then Abram bound the youth with belts and strap
And builded parapets and trenches there,
And stretched forth the knife to slay his son:
When lo! an angel called him out of heaven,
Saying, Lay not thy hand upon the lad,
Neither do anything to him. Behold,
A ram caught in the thicket by its horns;
Offer the Ram of Pride instead of him.
But the old man would not so, but slew his son. . .

WILFRED OWEN.

## Futility

Move him into the sun—
Gently its touch awoke him once,
At home, whispering of fields unsown.
Always it woke him, even in France,
Until this morning and this snow.
If anything might rouse him now
The kind old sun will know.

Think how it wakes the seeds—
Woke, once, the clays of a cold star.
Are limbs so dear-achieved, are sides
Full-nerved, still warm,—too hard to stir ?

WILFRED OWEN.

## Anthem for Doomed Youth

What passing-bells for these who die as cattle ?
   Only the monstrous anger of the guns.
   Only the stuttering rifles' rapid rattle
Can patter out their hasty orisons.
No mockeries for them; no prayer nor bells,
Nor any voice of mourning save the choirs—
The shrill, demented choirs—of wailing shells;
And bugles calling for them from sad shires.

What candles may be held to speed them all ?
   Not in the hands of boys, but in their eyes
Shall shine the holy glimmer of good-byes.
   The pallor of girls' brows shall be their pall;
Their flowers the tenderness of patient minds,
And each slow dusk a drawing-down of blinds.

WILFRED OWEN.

It seemed that out of the battle I escaped
Down some profound dull tunnel, long since
    scooped
Through granites which Titanic wars had groined.
Yet also there encumbered sleepers groaned,
Too fast in thought or death to be bestirred.
Then, as I probed them, one sprang up, and stared
With piteous recognition in fixed eyes,
Lifting distressful hands as if to bless.
And by his smile I knew that sullen hall;
With a thousand fears that vision's face was grained;
Yet no blood reached there from the upper ground,
And no guns thumped, or down the flues made
    moan.
" Strange, friend," I said, " here is no cause to
    mourn."
" None," said the other, " save the undone years,
The hopelessness. Whatever hope is yours,
Was my life also ; I went hunting wild
After the wildest beauty in the world,
Which lies not calm in eyes, or braided hair,
But mocks the steady running of the hour,
And if it grieves, grieves richlier than here.
For by my glee might many men have laughed,
And of my weeping something has been left,
Which must die now. I mean the truth untold,
The pity of war, the pity war distilled.
Now men will go content with what we spoiled.
Or, discontent, boil bloody, and be spilled.
They will be swift with swiftness of the tigress,

None will break ranks, though nations trek from
    progress.
Courage was mine, and I had mystery;
Wisdom was mine, and I had mastery;
To miss the march of this retreating world
Into vain citadels that are not walled.
Then, when much blood had clogged their chariot-
    wheels
I would go up and wash them from sweet wells,
Even with truths that lie too deep for taint.
I would have poured my spirit without stint
But not through wounds ; not on the cess of war.
Foreheads of men have bled where no wounds were.
I am the enemy you killed, my friend
I knew you in this dark; for so you frowned
Yesterday through me as you jabbed and killed.
I parried; but my hands were loath and cold.
Let us sleep now. . . ."

WILFRED OWEN.

(*This poem was found among the author's papers. It
ends on this strange note.*)

# The Veteran

## May, 1916

We came upon him sitting in the sun,
  Blinded by war, and left. And past the fence
There came young soldiers from the *Hand and
    Flower*,
  Asking advice of his experience.

And he said this, and that, and told them tales,
  And all the nightmares of each empty head
Blew into air; then, hearing us beside,
  " Poor chaps, how'd they know what it's like ? "
    he said.

And we stood there, and watched him as he sat,
  Turning his sockets where they went away,
Until it came to one of us to ask
  " And you're—how old ? "
        " Nineteen, the third of May."

MARGARET POSTGATE.

## *Præmaturi*

When men are old, and their friends die,
They are not so sad,
Because their love is running slow,
And cannot spring from the wound with so sharp a
     pain;
And they are happy with many memories,
And only a little while to be alone.

But we are young, and our friends are dead
Suddenly, and our quick love is torn in two;
So our memories are only hopes that came to nothing.
We are left alone like old men; we should be dead
—But there are years and years in which we shall
     still be young.

MARGARET POSTGATE.

Met ye my love?
Ye might in France have met him;
He has a wooing smile,
Who sees cannot forget him!
Met ye my love?—
—We shared full many a mile.

Saw ye my love?
In lands far-off he has been,
With his yellow-tinted hair,—
In Egypt such ye have seen,
Ye knew my love?—
—I was his brother there.

Heard ye my love?
My love ye must have heard,
For his voice when he will
Tinkles like cry of a bird;
Heard ye my love?—
—We sang on a Grecian hill.

Behold your love,
And how shall I forget him,
His smile, his hair, his song;
Alas, no maid shall get him
For all her love,
Where he sleeps a million strong.

FRANK PREWETT.

His wild heart beats with painful sobs,
His strained hands clench an ice-cold rifle,
His aching jaws grip a hot parched tongue,
And his wide eyes search unconsciously.

He cannot shriek.

Bloody saliva
Dribbles down his shapeless jacket.

I saw him stab
And stab again
A well-killed Boche.

This is the happy warrior,
This is he. . . .

HERBERT READ.

## "*We Shall Drink to Them that Sleep*"

CAMPBELL

Yes, you will do it, silently of course;
For after many a toast and much applause,
One is in love with silence, being hoarse,
—Such more than sorrow is your quiet's
    cause.

Yes, I can see you at it, in a room
Well-lit and warm, high-roofed and soft to the
    tread,
Satiate and briefly mindful of the tomb
With its poor victim of Teutonic lead.

Some unknown notability will rise,
Ridiculously solemn, glass abrim,
And say, "To our dear brethren in the
    skies,"—
Dim are all eyes, all glasses still more dim.

Your pledge of sorrow but a cup of cheer,
Your sole remark some witless platitude,
Such as, " Although it does not yet appear,
To suffer is the sole beatitude.

"Life has, of course, good moments such
    as this
(A glass of sherry we should never spurn),
But where our brethren are, 'tis perfect bliss;
Still, we are glad our lot was,—to return."

Yes, I can see you and can see the dead,
Keen-eyed at last for Truth, with gentle mirth
Intent. And having heard, smiling they said:
" Strange are our little comrades of the
earth."

ALEXANDER ROBERTSON.
*Corporal, 12th York and Lancasters.*

# To an Old Lady Seen at a Guest-house for Soldiers

Quiet thou didst stand at thine appointed place,
There was no press to purchase—younger grace
Attracts the youth of valour. Thou didst not know,
Like the old, kindly Marthas, to and fro
To haste. Yet one could say, " In thine I prize
The strength of calm that held in Mary's eyes."
And when they came, thy gracious smile so wrought
They knew that they were given, not that they
  bought.
Thou didst not tempt to vauntings and pretence
Was dumb before thy perfect woman's sense.
Blest who have seen, for they shall ever see
The radiance of thy benignity.

ALEXANDER ROBERTSON.
*Corporal, 12th York and Lancasters.*

## Killed in Action

Your " Youth "* has fallen from its shelf,
And you have fallen, you yourself.
They knocked a soldier on the head,
I mourn the poet who fell dead.
And yet I think it was by chance,
By oversight you died in France.
You were so poor an outward man,
So small against your spirit's span,
That Nature, being tired awhile,
Saw but your outward human pile;
And Nature, who would never let
A sun with light still in it set,
Before you even reached your sky,
In inadvertence let you die.

ISAAC ROSENBERG.

* " *Youth,*" *a volume of poems by I. Rosenberg.*

## Marching

*(As seen from the left file)*

My eyes catch ruddy necks
Sturdily pressed back—
All flaming pendulums, hands
Swing across the Khaki—
Mustard-coloured Khaki—
To the automatic feet.

We husband the ancient glory
In these bared necks and hands.
Not broke in the forge of Mars;
But a subtler brain beats iron
To shoe the hoofs of death
(Who paws dynamic air now).
Blind fingers loose an iron cloud
To rain immortal darkness
On strong eyes.

Isaac Rosenberg.

## Dead Man's Dump

The plunging limbers over the shattered
    track
Racketed with their rusty freight,
Stuck out like many crowns of thorns,
And the rusty stakes like sceptres old
To stay the flood of brutish men
Upon our brothers dear.


The wheels lurched over sprawled dead
But pained them not, though their bones
    crunched;
Their shut mouths made no moan,
They lie there huddled, friend and foeman,
Man born of man, and born of woman;
And shells go crying over them
From night till night and now.


Earth has waited for them,
All the time of their growth
Fretting for their decay:
Now she has them at last!
In the strength of her strength
Suspended—stopped and held.


What fierce imaginings their dark souls lit?
Earth! Have they gone into you?
Somewhere they must have gone,

And flung on your hard back
Is their souls' sack,
Emptied of God-ancestralled essences.
Who hurled them out ? Who hurled ?


None saw their spirits' shadow shake the
    grass,
Or stood aside for the half-used life to pass
Out of those doomed nostrils and the doomed
    mouth,
When the swift iron burning bee
Drained the wild honey of their youth.


What of us who, flung on the shrieking pyre,
Walk, our usual thoughts untouched,
Our lucky limbs as on ichor fed,
Immortal seeming ever ?
Perhaps when the flames beat loud on us,
A fear may choke in our veins
And the startled blood may stop.


The air is loud with death,
The dark air spurts with fire,
The explosions ceaseless are.
Timelessly now, some minutes past,
These dead strode time with vigorous life,
Till the shrapnel called " An end ! "
But not to all. In bleeding pangs
Some borne on stretchers dreamed of home,
Dear things, war-blotted from their hearts.

A man's brains splattered on
A stretcher-bearer's face;
His shook shoulders slipped their load,
But when they bent to look again
The drowning soul was sunk too deep
For human tenderness.


They left this dead with the older dead,
Stretched at the cross roads.


Burnt black by strange decay
Their sinister faces lie,
The lid over each eye;
The grass and coloured clay
More motion have than they,
Joined to the great sunk silences.


Here is one not long dead.
His dark hearing caught our far wheels,
And the choked soul stretched weak hands
To reach the living word the far wheels said;
The blood-dazed intelligence beating for light,
Crying through the suspense of the far torturing
    wheels
Swift for the end to break
Or the wheels to break,
Cried as the tide of the world broke over his sight,
" Will they come ?  Will they ever come ? "
Even as the mixed hoofs of the mules,

The quivering-bellied mules,
And the rushing wheels all mixed
With his tortured upturned sight.

So we crashed round the bend,
We heard his weak scream,
We heard his very last sound,
And our wheels grazed his dead face.

                    ISAAC ROSENBERG.

## Raindrops

Raindrops falling,
Falling on the reddened grass
Where through the night battle held full sway,
Like Tears of God that drop in pity, then pass
To wash our guilt away.

H. SMALLEY SARSON.
*Private, Canadian Contingent.*

## Base Details

If I were fierce and bald and short of breath
    I'd live with scarlet Majors at the Base,
And speed glum heroes up the line to death.
    You'd see me with my puffy petulant face,
Guzzling and gulping in the best hotel,
    Reading the Roll of Honour. " Poor young
        chap,"
I'd say—" I used to know his father well;
    Yes, we've lost heavily in this last scrap."
And when the war is done and youth stone dead,
I'd toddle safely home and die—in bed.

SIEGFRIED SASSOON.

1917.

## " Blighters "

The House is crammed: tier beyond tier they grin
And cackle at the Show, while prancing ranks
Of harlots shrill the chorus, drunk with din;
" We're sure the Kaiser loves the dear old Tanks! "

I'd like to see a Tank come down the stalls,
Lurching to rag-time, or " Home, sweet Home,"—
And there'd be no more jokes in music-halls
To mock the riddled corpses round Bapaume.

SIEGFRIED SASSOON.

1916.

## Glory of Women

You love us when we're heroes, home on leave,
Or wounded in a mentionable place.
You worship decorations; you believe
That chivalry redeems the war's disgrace.
You make us shells. You listen with delight,
By tales of dirt and danger fondly thrilled.
You crown our distant ardours while we fight,
And mourn our laurelled memories when we're
       killed.

You can't believe that British troops " retire "
When hell's last horror breaks them, and they run,
Trampling the terrible corpses—blind with blood.
*O German mother dreaming by the fire,*
*While you are knitting socks to send your son*
*His face is trodden deeper in the mud.*

                          SIEGFRIED SASSOON.
  1917.

We'd gained our first objective hours before
While dawn broke like a face with blinking eyes,
Pallid, unshaved and thirsty, blind with smoke.
Things seemed all right at first.  We held their line,
With bombers posted, Lewis guns well placed,
And clink of shovels deepening the shallow trench.
The place was rotten with dead; green clumsy legs
High-booted, sprawled and grovelled along the saps;
And trunks, face downwards, in the sucking mud,
Wallowed like trodden sand-bags loosely filled;
And naked sodden buttocks, mats of hair,
Bulged, clotted heads slept in the plastering slime.

And then the rain began,—the jolly old rain!
A yawning soldier knelt against the bank,
Staring across the morning blear with fog;
He wondered when the Allemands would get busy;
And then, of course, they started with five-nines
Traversing, sure as fate, and never a dud.
Mute in the clamour of shells he watched them
    burst,
Spouting dark earth and wire with gusts from hell,
While posturing giants dissolved in drifts of smoke.
He crouched and flinched, dizzy with galloping fear,
Sick for escape,—loathing the strangled horror
And butchered, frantic gestures of the dead.

An officer came blundering down the trench:
" Stand-to and man the fire-step!"  On he
    went . . .

138

asping and bawling, "Fire-step . . . Counter-
    attack!"
hen the haze lifted. Bombing on the right
own the old sap: machine-guns on the left;
nd stumbling figures looking out in front.
O Christ, they're coming at us!" Bullets spat,
nd he remembered his rifle . . . rapid fire . . .
nd started blazing wildly. . . . Then a bang
rumpled and spun him sideways, knocked him out
o grunt and wriggle: none heeded him; he
    choked
nd fought the flapping veils of smothering gloom,
ost in a blurred confusion of yells and groans . . .
own, and down, and down, he sank and drowned,
leeding to death. The counter-attack had failed.

SIEGFRIED SASSOON.

## Dreamers

Soldiers are citizens of death's grey land,
   Drawing no dividend from time's to-morrows.
In the great hour of destiny they stand,
   Each with his feuds, and jealousies, and sorrow
Soldiers are sworn to action; they must win
   Some flaming, fatal climax with their lives.
Soldiers are dreamers; when the guns begin
   They think of firelit homes, clean beds, and wive

I see them in foul dug-outs, gnawed by rats,
   And in the ruined trenches, lashed with rain,
Dreaming of things they did with balls and bats,
   And mocked by hopeless longing to regain
Bank-holidays, and picture shows, and spats,
   And going to the office in the train.

SIEGFRIED SASSOON.

## The One-Legged Man

Propped on a stick he viewed the August weald;
Square orchard trees and oasts with painted cowls;
A homely, tangled hedge, a corn-stooked field,
With sound of barking dogs and farmyard fowls.

And he'd come home again to find it more
Desirable than ever it was before.
How right it seemed that he should reach the span
Of comfortable years allowed to man!
Splendid to eat and sleep and choose a wife,
Safe with his wound, a citizen of life.
He hobbled blithely through the garden gate,
And thought: " Thank God they had to amputate! "

Siegfried Sassoon.

## To One Who was with Me in the War

It was too long ago—that Company which we serv
    with . . .
We call it back in visual fragments, you and I,
Who seem, ourselves, like relics casually preserv
    with
Our mindfulness of old bombardments when t
    sky
With blundering din blinked cavernous,
                    Yet a sense of power
Invaded us when, recapturing an ungodly hour
Of ante-zero crisis, in one thought we've met
To stand in some redoubt of Time—to share aga
All but the actual witness of the flare-lit rain,
All but the living presences who haunt us yet
With gloom-patrolling eyes.
                    Remembering, we forget
Much that was monstrous, much that clogged ou
    souls with clay
When hours were guides who led us by the longe
    way—
And when the worst had been endured could sti
    disclose
Another worst to thwart us . . .
                  We forget our fear . . .
And, while the uncouth Event begins to lour le
    near,
Discern the mad magnificence whose storm-ligh
    throws
Wild shadows on these after-thoughts that sen
    your brain

ack beyond Peace, exploring sunken ruinous roads.
our brain, with files of flitting forms hump-backed
 with loads,
n its own helmet hears the tinkling drops of rain,—
ollows to an end some night-relief, and strangely
 sees
he quiet no-man's-land of daybreak, jagg'd with
 trees
hat loom like giant Germans . . .
                    I'll go with you, then,
ince you must play this game of ghosts. At
 listening-posts
Ve'll peer across dim craters; joke with jaded men
Vhose names we've long forgotten. (Stoop low
 there; it's the place
he sniper enfilades.) Round the next bay you'll
 meet
. drenched platoon-commander; chilled he drums
 his feet
In squelching duck-boards; winds his wrist watch;
 turns his head,
nd shows you how you looked—your ten-years-
 vanished face,
Ioping the War will end next week . . .
                    What's that you said ?

SIEGFRIED SASSOON.

143

## " *I Have a Rendezvous with Death* "

I have a rendezvous with Death
At some disputed barricade,
When Spring comes back with rustling shade
And apple-blossoms fill the air—
I have a rendezvous with Death
When Spring brings back blue days and fair.

It may be he shall take my hand
And lead me into his dark land
And close my eyes and quench my breath—
It may be I shall pass him still.
I have a rendezvous with Death
On some scarred slope of battered hill,
When Spring comes round again this year
And the first meadow-flowers appear.

God knows 'twere better to be deep
Pillowed in silk and scented down,
Where Love throbs out in blissful sleep,
Pulse nigh to pulse, and breath to breath,
Where hushed awakenings are dear. . . .
But I've a rendezvous with Death
At midnight in some flaming town,
When Spring trips north again this year,
And I to my pledged word am true,
I shall not fail that rendezvous.

ALAN SEEGER.

## All the Hills and Vales

All the hills and vales along
Earth is bursting into song,
And the singers are the chaps
Who are going to die perhaps.
      O sing, marching men,
      Till the valleys ring again.
      Give your gladness to earth's keeping,
      So be glad, when you are sleeping.

Cast away regret and rue,
Think what you are marching to.
Little live, great pass.
Jesus Christ and Barabbas
Were found the same day.
This died, that went his way.
      So sing with joyful breath.
      For why, you are going to death.
      Teeming earth will surely store
      All the gladness that you pour.

Earth that never doubts nor fears,
Earth that knows of death, not tears,
Earth that bore with joyful ease
Hemlock for Socrates,
Earth that blossomed and was glad
'Neath the cross that Christ had,
Shall rejoice and blossom too
When the bullet reaches you.

Wherefore, men, marching
On the road to death, sing;
Pour your gladness on earth's head,
So be merry, so be dead.

From the hills and valleys earth
Shouts back the sound of mirth,
Tramp of feet and lilt of song
Ringing all the road along.
All the music of their going,
Ringing-swinging, glad song-throwing,
Earth will echo still, when foot
Lies numb and voice mute.
On, marching men, on
To the gates of death with song.
Sow your gladness for earth's reaping,
So you may be glad, though sleeping.
Strew your gladness on earth's bed,
So be merry, so be dead.

C. H. SORLEY.

The heat came down and sapped away my powers.
  The laden heat came down and drowned my
     brain,
All through the weight of overcoming hours
           I felt the rain.

Then suddenly I saw what more to see
  I never thought: old things renewed, retrieved,
The rain that fell in England fell on me,
           And I believed.

C. H. SORLEY.

## Before Action

Over the down the road goes winding,
  A ribbon of white in the corn—
The green, young corn. O, the joy of binding
  The sheaves some harvest morn!

But we are called to another reaping,
  A harvest that will not wait.
The sheaves will be green. O, the world of weeping
  Of those without the gate!

For the road we go they may not travel,
  Nor share our harvesting;
But watch and weep. O, to unravel
  The riddle of this thing!

Yet over the down the white road leading
  Calls; and who lags behind?
Stout are our hearts; but O, the bleeding
  Of hearts we may not bind!

J. E. STEWART.
*M.C., Capt., Border Regiment*

*Somme, July,* 1916.

# Courage

I was afraid of Fear,
   Not of the foe;
And when I thought that those I hold most dear
   My craven soul would know
And turn away ashamed, who praised before,
   Ashamed and deep distressed to find it so,
I was afraid the more.

Lo, when I joined the fight,
   And bared my breast
To all the darts of that wild hellish night,
   I, only, stood the test,
For Fear, which I had feared, deserved then,
   And forward blithely at the foe I prest
King of myself again.

ENVOY

Blessed be God above
   For His sweet care,
Who heard the prayers of those who most I love
   And my poor suppliance there,
Who brought me forth in life and limb all whole,
   Who blessed my powers with his Divine repair,
And gave me back my soul!

J. E. STEWART.
*M.C., Capt., Border Regiment.*

## A Lark Above the Trenches

Hushed is the shriek of hurtling shells: and har
Somewhere within that bit of deep blue sky,
Grand in his loneliness, his ecstasy,
His lyric wild and free, carols a lark.
I in the trench, he lost in heaven afar;
I dream of love, its ecstasy he sings;
Both lure my soul to love till, like a star,
It flashes into life:  O tireless wings
That beat love's message into melody—
A song that touches in this place remote
Gladness supreme in its undying note,
And stirs to life the soul of memory—
'Tis strange that while you're beating into life
Men here below are plunged in sanguine strife.

JOHN WILLIAM STREETS.

*Sergt., 12th York and Lancasters (B.E.F., Fran*
*Wounded and Missing, July, 19*

Green gardens in Laventie!
    Soldiers only know the street
Where the mud is churned and splashed about
    by battle-wending feet;
And yet beside one stricken house there is a glimpse
       of grass,
    Look for it when you pass.


Beyond the Church whose pitted spire
    Seems balanced on a strand
Of swaying stone and tottering brick
    Two roofless ruins stand,
And here behind the wreckage where the back wall
      should have been
    We found a garden green.


The grass was never trodden on,
    The little path of gravel
Was overgrown with celandine,
    No other folk did travel
Along its weedy surface, but the nimble-footed
      mouse
    Running from house to house.


So all among the vivid blades
    Of soft and tender grass

We lay, nor heard the limber wheels
    That pass and ever pass,
In noisy continuity until their stony rattle
    Seems in itself a battle.


At length we rose up from this ease
    Of tranquil happy mind,
And searched the garden's little length
    A fresh pleasaunce to find;
And there, some yellow daffodils and jasmine
    hanging high
    Did rest the tired eye.


The fairest and most fragrant
    Of the many sweets we found,
Was a little bush of Daphne flower
    Upon a grassy mound,
And so thick were the blossoms set and so divine
    the scent
    That we were well content.


Hungry for spring I bent my head,
    The perfume fanned my face,
And all my soul was dancing
    In that lovely little place,
Dancing with a measured step from wrecked and
    shattered towns
    Away . . . upon the Downs.

I saw green banks of daffodil,
　　Slim poplars in the breeze,
Great tan-brown hares in gusty March
　　A-couching on the leas:
And meadows with their glittering streams and
　　　silver scurrying dace,
　　Home—what a perfect place!

EDWARD WYNDHAM TENNANT.

*Belgium, March,* 1916.

## No One Cares Less Than I

" No one cares less than I,
Nobody knows but God,
Whether I am destined to lie
Under a foreign clod,"
Were the words I made to the bugle call in
    the morning.

But laughing, storming, scorning,
Only the bugles know
What the bugles say in the morning,
And they do not care, when they blow
The call that I heard and made words to early
    this morning.

EDWARD THOMAS.

## A Private

This ploughman dead in battle slept out of doors
Many a frozen night, and merrily
Answered staid drinkers, good bedman, and all bores
" At Mrs. Greenland's Hawthorn Bush," said he,
" I slept." None knew which bush. Above the town,
Beyond " The Drover," a hundred spot the down
In Wiltshire. And where now at last he sleeps
More sound in France—that, too, he secret keeps.

EDWARD THOMAS.

## 1925

To-day we must recall abysmal follies
That have bequeathed our friends to flies and sour
    clay,
That bent the air with groaning flights of steel
Or sweetened it with a shell's livid breath,
Turned wholesome plains and gentle lakes to filth,
Tore up our continent in unscavenged belts
Through   cross-edged   meadows   and   afforested
    heights
Where the guns crouched in pits and shouted
Lunatic judgment in dull obedience.
We must remember the weary stand-to
Of millions, pale in corpse-infected mist,
The mad, and those turned monsters, or castrated
In one red, hideous moment; and how, unseen
Dark Mania sat in offices, and designed
New schemes for shambles, learning year by year,
Painfully, secretly, to degrade the world.

SHERARD VINES.

## Christ in Flanders

We had forgotten You, or very nearly—
You did not seem to touch us very
    nearly—
    Of course we thought about You now
    and then;
Especially in any time of trouble—
We knew that You were good in time of
    trouble—
    But we are very ordinary men.

And there were always other things to
    think of—
There's lots of things a man has got to
    think of—
    His work, his home, his pleasure, and
    his wife;
And so we only thought of You on
    Sunday—
Sometimes, perhaps, not even on a
    Sunday—
    Because there's always lots to fill one's
    life.

And, all the while, in street or lane or
    byway—
In country lane, in city street, or byway—
    You walked among us, and we did not
    see.
Your Feet were bleeding as You walked
    our pavements—

How *did* we miss Your Footprints on
    our pavements ?—
    Can there be other folk as blind as
      we ?


*Now* we remember; over here in
    Flanders—
(It isn't strange to think of You in
    Flanders)—
    This hideous warfare seems to make
    things clear.
We never thought about You much in
    England—
But now that we are far away from
    England—
    We have no doubts, we know that
    You are here.


You helped us pass the jest along the
    trenches—
Where, in cold blood, we waited in the
    trenches—
    You touched its ribaldry and made
    it fine.
You stood beside us in our pain and
    weakness—
We're glad to think You understand our
    weakness—
    Somehow it seems to help us not to
    whine.

We think about You kneeling in the
    Garden—
Ah ! God ! the agony of that dread
    Garden—
    We know You prayed for us upon the
      Cross.
If anything could make us glad to bear
    it—
'Twould be the knowledge that You
    willed to bear it—
    Pain—death—the uttermost of human
      loss.

Though we forgot You—You will not
    forget us—
We feel so sure that You will not forget
    us—
    But stay with us until this dream is
      past.
And so we ask for courage, strength, and
    pardon—
Especially, I think, we ask for pardon—
    And that You'll stand beside us to the
      last.

L. W.

# The Casualty Clearing Station

A bowl of daffodils,
A crimson-quilted bed,
Sheets and pillows white as snow—
White and gold and red—
And sisters moving to and fro,
With soft and silent tread.

So all my spirit fills
With pleasure infinite,
And all the feathered wings of rest
Seem flocking from the radiant West
To bear me thro' the night.

See, how they close me in,
They, and the sisters' arms,
One eye is closed, the other lid
Is watching how my spirit slid
Toward some red-roofed farms,
And having crept beneath them, slept
Secure from war's alarms.

GILBERT WATERHOUSE.
*Lieut., 2nd Essex.*

# The Night Patrol

*France, March,* 1916.

Over the top! The wire's thin here, unbarbed
Plain rusty coils, not staked, and low enough:
Full of old tins, though—" When you're
    through, all three,
Aim quarter left for fifty yards or so,
Then straight for that new piece of German
    wire;
See if it's thick, and listen for a while
For sounds of working; don't run any risks;
About an hour; now, over! "
                    And we placed
Our hands on the topmost sand-bags, leapt,
    and stood
A second with curved backs, then crept to the
    wire,
Wormed ourselves tinkling through, glanced
    back, and dropped.
The sodden ground was splashed with shallow
    pools,
And tufts of crackling cornstalks, two years
    old,
No man had reaped, and patches of spring
    grass,
Half-seen, as rose and sank the flares, were
    strewn
With the wrecks of our attack: the bandoliers,
Packs, rifles, bayonets, belts, and haversacks,
Shell fragments, and the huge whole forms of
    shells

Shot fruitlessly—and everywhere the dead.
Only the dead were always present—present
As a vile sickly smell of rottenness;
The rustling stubble and the early grass,
The slimy pools—the dead men stank through
    all,
Pungent and sharp; as bodies loomed before,
And as we passed, they stank; then dulled
    away
To that vague factor, all encompassing,
Infecting earth and air. They lay, all clothed,
Each in some new and piteous attitude
That we well marked to guide us back; as he,
Outside our wire, that lay on his back and
    crossed
His legs Crusader-wise; I smiled at that,
And thought of Elia and his Temple Church.
From him, a quarter left, lay a small corpse,
Down in a hollow, huddled as in bed,
That one of us put his hand on unawares.
Next was a bunch of half a dozen men
All blown to bits, an archipelago
Of corrupt fragments, vexing to us three,
Who had no light to see by, save the flares.
On such a trail, so lit, for ninety yards
We crawled on belly and elbows, till we saw,
Instead of lumpish dead before our eyes,
The stakes and crosslines of the German
    wire.
We lay in shelter of the last dead man,
Ourselves as dead, and heard their shovels
    ring

Turning the earth, their talk and cough at
    times.
A sentry fired and a machine-gun spat;
They shot a flare above us, when it fell
And spluttered out in the pools of No Man's
    Land,
We turned and crawled past the remembered
    dead:
Past him and him, and them and him, until,
For he lay some way apart, we caught the
    scent
Of the Crusader and slid past his legs,
And through the wire and home, and got our
    rum.

ARTHUR GRAEME WEST.

## At Last Post

Come home!—Come home!
The winds are at rest in the restful trees;
At rest are the waves of the sundown seas;
And home—they're home—
The wearied hearts and the broken lives—
At home! At ease!

WALTER LIGHOWLER WILKINSON.
*Lieut., 8th Argyll and Sutherland Highlanders*
*(Killed on Vimy Ridge, April 9, 1917).*

*B.E.F., France.*

# From a Flemish Graveyard

## January, 1915

A year hence may the grass that waves
O'er English men in Flemish graves,
Coating this clay with green of peace
And softness of a year's increase,
Be kind and lithe as English grass
To bend and nod as the winds pass;
It was for grass on English hills
These bore too soon the last of ills.

And may the wind be brisk and clean,
And singing cheerfully between
The bents a pleasant-burdened song
To cheer these English dead along;
For English songs and English winds
Are they that bred these English minds.

And may the circumstantial trees
Dip, for these dead ones, in the breeze,
And make for them their silver play
Of spangled boughs each shiny day.
Thus may these look above, and see
And hear the wind in grass and tree,
And watch a lark in heaven stand,
And think themselves in their own land.

IOLO ANEURIN WILLIAMS.

## Magpies in Picardy

The magpies in Picardy
Are more than I can tell.
They flicker down the dusty roads
And cast a magic spell
On the men who march through Picardy,
Through Picardy to hell.

(The blackbird flies with panic,
The swallow goes like light,
The finches move like ladies,
The owl floats by at night;
But the great and flashing magpie
He flies as artists might.)

A magpie in Picardy
Told me secret things—
Of the music in white feathers,
And the sunlight that sings
And dances in deep shadows—
He told me with his wings.

(The hawk is cruel and rigid,
He watches from a height;
The rook is slow and sombre,
The robin loves to fight;
But the great and flashing magpie
He flies as lovers might.)

He told me that in Picardy,
An age ago or more,

While all his fathers still were eggs,
Those dusty highways bore
Brown singing soldiers marching out
Through Picardy to war.

T. P. CAMERON WILSON.

## England—April, 1918

Last night the North flew at the throat of Spring
With spite to tear her greening banners down,
Tossing the elm-trees tender tassels brown,
The virgin blossom of sloe burdening
With colder snow; beneath his frosty sting
Patient, the newly-wakened woods were bowed
By drowned fields where stormy waters flowed:
Yet, on the thorn, I heard a blackbird sing . . .
" Too late, too late," he sang, " this wintry spite;
For molten snow will feed the springing grass:
The tide of life, it floweth with the year."
O England, England, thou that standest upright
Against the tide of death, the bad days pass:
Know, by this miracle, that summer is near.

FRANCIS BRETT YOUNG.

# The Pavement

In bitter London's heart of stone,
　　Under the lamplight's shielded glare,
I saw a soldier's body thrown
　　Unto the drabs that traffic there

Pacing the pavements with slow feet:
　　Those old pavements whose blown dust
Throttles the hot air of the street,
　　And the darkness smells of lust.

The chaste moon, with equal glance,
　　Looked down on the mad world, astare
At those who conquered in sad France
　　And those who perished in Leicester Square.

And in her light his lips were pale:
　　Lips that love had moulded well:
Out of the jaws of Passchendæle
　　They had sent him to this nether hell.

I had no stone of scorn to fling,
　　For I know not how the wrong began—
But I had seen a hateful thing
　　Masked in the dignity of man:

And hate and sorrow and hopeless anger
　　Swept my heart, as the winds that sweep
Angrily through the leafless hanger
　　When winter rises from the deep. . . .

　　·　　　·　　　·　　　·　　　·

169

I would that war were what men dream:
A crackling fire, a cleansing flame,
That it might leap and space between
And lap up London and its shame.

FRANCIS BRETT YOUNG.

Into that dry and most desolate place
With heavy gait they dragged the stretcher in
And laid him on the bloody ground: the din
Of Maxim fire ceased not. I raised his head,
And looked into his face,
And saw that he was dead.
Saw beneath matted curls the broken skin
That let the bullet in;
And saw the limp, lithe limbs, the smiling mouth . . .
Ah, may we smile at death
As bravely . . .) the curv'd lips that no more drouth
Should blacken, and no sweetly stirring breath
Mildly displace.
So I covered the calm face
And stripped the shirt from his firm breast, and
       there,
A zinc identity disc, a bracelet of elephant hair
I found. . . . Ah, God, how deep it stings
This unendurable pity of small things!

But more than this I saw,
That dead stranger welcoming, more than the raw
And brutal havoc of war.
England I saw, the mother from whose side
He came hither and died, she at whose hems he had
       play'd,
In whose quiet womb his body and soul were made.
That pale, estranged flesh that we bowed over
Had breathed the scent in summer of white clover;
Dreamed her cool fading nights, her twilights long,

And days as careless as a blackbird's song
Heard in the hush of eve, when midges' wings
Make a thin music, and the night-jar spins.
(For it is summer, I thought, in England now . . .
And once those forward gazing eyes had seen
Her lovely living green: that blackened brow
Cool airs, from those blue hills moving, had fann'd—
Breath of that holy land
Whither my soul aspireth without despair:
In the broken brain had many a lovely word
Awakened magical echoes of things heard,
Telling of love and laughter and low voices,
And tales in which the English heart rejoices
In vanishing visions of childhood and its glories:
Old-fashioned nursery rhymes and fairy stories:
Words that only an English tongue could tell.

And the firing died away; and the night fell
On our battle. Only in the sullen sky
A prairie fire, with huge fantastic flame
Leapt, lighting dark clouds charged with thunder.
And my heart was sick with shame
That there, in death, he should lie,
Crying: " Oh, why am I alive, I wonder ? "

In a dream I saw war riding the land:
Stark rode she, with bowed eyes, against the glare
Of sack'd cities smouldering in the dark,
A tired horse, lean, with outreaching head,
And hid her face of dread . . .
Yet, in my passion would I look on her,
Crying, O hark,

Thou pale one, whom now men say bearest the
  scythe
Of God, that iron scythe forged by his thunder
For reaping of nations overripened, fashioned
Upon the clanging anvil whose sparks, flying
In a starry night, dying, fall hereunder . . .
But she, she heeded not my cry impassioned
Nor turned her face of dread,
Urging the tired horse, with outreaching head,
O thou, cried I, who choosest for thy going
These bloomy meadows of youth, these flowery ways
Whereby no influence strays
Ruder than a cold wind blowing,
Or beating needles of rain,
Why must thou ride again
Ruthless among the pastures yet unripened,
Crushing their beauty in thine iron track
Downtrodden, ravish'd in thy following flame,
Parched and black ?
But she, she stayed not in her weary haste
Nor turned her face; but fled:
And where she passed the lands lay waste . . .

And now I cannot tell whither she rideth:
But tired, tired rides she.
Yet know I well why her dread face she hideth:
She is pale and faint to death.  Yea, her day faileth,
Nor all her blood, nor all her frenzy burning,
Nor all her hate availeth:
For she passeth out of sight
Into that night
From which none, none returneth

173

To waste the meadows of youth,
Nor vex thine eyelids, Routhe,
O sorrowful sister, soother of our sorrow.
And a hope within me springs
That fair will be the morrow,
And that charred plain,
Those flowery meadows, shall rejoice at last
In a sweet, clean
Freshness, as when the green
Grass springeth, where the prairie fire hath passe

Francis Brett Young.

## The Gift

Marching on Tanga, marching the parch'd plain
Of wavering spear-grass past Pangani River,
England came to me—me who had always ta'en
But never given before—England, the giver,
In a vision of three poplar-trees that shiver
On still evenings of summer, after rain,
By Slapton Ley, where reed-beds start and quiver
When scarce a ripple moves the upland grain.
Then I thanked God that now I had suffered pain,
And, as the parch'd plain, thirst, and lain awake
Shivering all night through till cold daybreak:
In that I count these sufferings my gain
And her acknowledgment. Nay, more, would fain
Suffer as many more for her sweet sake.

FRANCIS BRETT YOUNG.

# ACKNOWLEDGMENTS

The Editor's thanks are due to the authors and publisher
of the following poems :—

*Barrage, Bombardment, Machine Guns,* and *A Moment's
Interlude,* by Richard Aldington, from *Collected Poems.*
Published by George Allen & Unwin, Ltd.

*Nox Mortis,* by Paul Bewsher, from *The Bombing of
Bruges.* Published by Hodder & Stoughton, Ltd.

*For the Fallen,* by Laurence Binyon. Reprinted by
permission of the author and *The Times.*

*Third Ypres* and *The Zonnebeke Road,* by Edmund
Blunden, from *Undertones of War.* Published by R.
Cobden-Sanderson, Ltd.

*Night Flying, Over the Dead,* and *Secret Treaties,* by
Frederick V. Branford, from *Titans and Gods.* Published
by Christophers.

*The Soldier,* by Rupert Brooke. Reprinted by permission
of the Literary Executor of Rupert Brooke and Sidgwick
& Jackson, Ltd.

*Guns of Verdun,* by P. R. Chalmers. Reprinted by
permission of the Proprietors of *Punch.*

" *On the Wings of the Morning,*" by Jeffery Day, from
*Poems and Rhymes.* Reprinted by permission of G. D. Day,
Esq., and Sidgwick & Jackson, Ltd.

*The Turkish Trench Dog,* by Geoffrey Dearmer. Published by William Heinemann, Ltd.

*Five Souls,* by W. N. Ewer.

*The Stars in their Courses,* by John Freeman. Reprinted
by permission of Mrs. G. Freeman.

*Youth's Own* and *The Bells of Peace,* by John Galsworthy.
Published by William Heinemann, Ltd.

*The Joke* and *The Lament,* by Wilfred Wilson Gibson,
from *Collected Poems,* 1905-1925. Published by Macmillan
& Co., Ltd.

*Summer and Sorrow*, by A. B. Gillespie. Reprinted by permission of the Proprietors of *Punch*.

*Corporal Stare* and *Two Fusiliers*, by Robert Graves. Published by William Heinemann, Ltd.

*Into Battle*, by Julian Grenfell. Reprinted by permission of Lady Desborough.

*Song of Pain and Beauty* and *To the Poet Before Battle*, by Ivor Gurney, from *Severn and Somme*. Published by Sidgwick & Jackson, Ltd.

*In Time of "The Breaking of Nations,"* by Thomas Hardy, from *The Collected Poems of Thomas Hardy*. Reprinted by permission of the author's Executors and Macmillan & Co., Ltd.

*Epitaph* and *Gonnehem*, by F. W. Harvey, from *A Gloucestershire Lad*, and *The Stranger* and *To the Devil on His Appalling Decadence*, by F. W. Harvey, from *Gloucestershire Friends*. Published by Sidgwick & Jackson, Ltd.

*After the Battle*, by A. P. Herbert, from *The Bomber Gipsy*. Published by Methuen & Co., Ltd.

*A Solus Ortus Cardine . . .* and *The Iron Music*, by Ford Madox Hueffer, from *On Heaven*. Published by John Lane, The Bodley Head, Limited.

*"For All We Have and Are,"* by Rudyard Kipling, from *The Years Between*. Published by Methuen & Co., Ltd.

*In France*, by Francis Ledwidge. Reprinted by permission of The Rt. Hon. Lord Dunsany. Published by Herbert Jenkins, Ltd.

*In Flanders Fields*, by John McCrae. Reprinted by permission of the Proprietors of *Punch*.

*"Il Est Cocu—Le Chef De Gare,"* by H. S. Mackintosh. Reprinted from *The London Mercury*.

*The Nurse*, by Miss G. M. Mitchell. Reprinted by permission of the Proprietors of *Punch*.

*Commandered*, by L. G. Moberley. Reprinted by permission of the Proprietors of *Punch*.

*The Flower of Battle*, by R. H. Mottram, from *Poems Old and New*. Published by Gerald Duckworth & Co., Ltd.

*Anthem for Doomed Youth, Dulce et Decorum Est, Futility, Parable of the Old Men and the Young,* and *Strange Meeting*, by Wilfred Owen. Published by Chatto & Windus.

*Præmaturi* and *The Veteran*, by Margaret Postgate.

*Voices of Women*, by Frank Prewett. Published by The Hogarth Press.

*The Happy Warrior*, by Herbert Read, from *The Scene of War*. Published by Faber & Faber, Ltd.

*Dead Man's Dump, Killed in Action*, and *Marching*, by Isaac Rosenberg. Published by Wm. Heinemann, Ltd. Reprinted by permission of Mrs. Wynick.

*Base Details, Blighters, Counter Attack, Dreamers, Glory of Women, The One-Legged Man*, and *To One Who Was With Me in the War*, by Siegfried Sassoon. Published by William Heinemann, Ltd.

"*I have a Rendezvous with Death*," by Alan Seeger. Published by Constable & Co.

*German Rain* and *All the Hills and Vales*, by C. H. Sorley. Published by The Cambridge University Press.

*Home Thoughts in Laventie*, by Edward Wyndham Tennant. Reprinted by permission of Lord Glenconner.

*A Private*, and *No One Cares Less Than I*, by Edward Thomas, from *Collected Poems*. Published by Ingpen & Grant.

*War Commemoration*, 1925, by Sherard Vines, from *The Pyramid*. Published by R. Cobden-Sanderson, Ltd.

*Christ in Flanders*, by L. W. Reprinted from *The Spectator*.

*The Night Patrol*, by Arthur Graeme West, from *The Diary of a Dead Officer*. Published by George Allen & Unwin, Ltd.

*From a Flemish Graveyard*, by Iolo Aneurin Williams.

*Magpies in Picardy*, by T. P. Cameron Wilson. Published by The Poetry Bookshop.

*England—April*, 1918, *The Gift, On a Subaltern Killed in Action*, and *The Pavement*, by Francis Brett Young, from *Poems*, 1916-1918. Published by Wm. Collins, Sons & Co., Ltd.

The Editor's thanks are also due to Messrs. Erskine Macdonald, Ltd., for their kind permission to include certain poems.

# INDEX OF AUTHORS

181

185

# INDEX OF FIRST LINES

Ren 245
M M R.

LONDON AND GLASGOW: COLLINS' CLEAR-TYPE PRESS